THE PHONETICS OF FRENCH

A PRACTICAL HANDBOOK

BY
LILIAS E. ARMSTRONG
LATE SENIOR LECTURER IN PHONETICS, UNIVERSITY COLLEGE, LONDON

WITH A FOREWORD BY
DANIEL JONES
EMERITUS PROFESSOR OF PHONETICS IN THE UNIVERSITY OF LONDON

LONDON
G BELL AND SONS, LTD
1964

First published 1932
Reprinted 1943, 1947, 1949, 1951, 1955, 1959, 1962, 1964

PRINTED IN GREAT BRITAIN BY
JOHN DICKENS AND CO LTD, NORTHAMPTON

FOREWORD

By Daniel Jones, Professor of Phonetics at
University College, London

IT is with much pleasure that I have accepted
Messrs. Bell's invitation to write a foreword to this
book, since I consider the work to be one of special
excellence and it supplies a need that has been long felt.

Miss Armstrong is particularly well qualified for
writing a book of this description. She is one of the
ablest phoneticians known to me. Moreover, she had
seven years' experience as a teacher of French in schools
before she was appointed to her present post at
University College, London (which she has held since
1918). Consequently she has had unique opportunities
of becoming familiar with the needs of every type of
teacher and pupil. The result is, as might be expected,
a book which is scientifically accurate, and at the same
time thoroughly practical from beginning to end.

All the essentials of French phonetic theory are to
be found in this book, together with a skilled and detailed
treatment of the pronunciation mistakes of English
learners and methods of acquiring correct pronunciation.
Much of the material is new, and it has all stood the
test of many years' practical application. The whole
is set out with a lucidity rarely found in books of this
nature. On every page one sees the hand of the expert
practical teacher. The value of the book is enhanced

by the inclusion of large numbers of examples illustrating each feature of pronunciation, and of diagrams showing the tongue-positions of all the important sounds.

Altogether I regard this book as a most important contribution to phonetic literature ; it should be in the hands of every teacher and student of spoken French.

DANIEL JONES

June, 1932

PREFACE

I HERE express my indebtedness to Professor Daniel Jones for much more than permission to use Diagram 1, taken from the 1932 edition of his *Outline of English Phonetics* ; and to Miss H. Coustenoble for kindly reading through the proofs and providing me with helpful notes.

Acknowledgments are due to Messrs. Plon, Paris, who have granted me permission to include a phonetic transcription of Chapter IX of *Mon Petit Trott*, by André Lichtenberger ; and to Messrs. Calmann-Lévy for permission to make a phonetic transcription of two extracts form *Pâques d'Islande*, by Anatole Le Braz.

The mouth-diagrams are intended to be no more than simple outlines such as can be quickly drawn to serve as blackboard sketches.

LILIAS E. ARMSTRONG

UNIVERSITY COLLEGE
LONDON
May, 1932

CONTENTS

CHAPTER I

INTRODUCTORY

Object of the Book

1. The object of this book is a practical one: it is to help English students of French pronunciation, and especially teachers of French pronunciation in our Central and Secondary schools.

2. Pronunciation is essentially an oral thing and cannot be studied adequately from a book. But a book written on practical lines can help if it is properly used. The reader is asked to *say aloud* all the isolated sounds and groups of sounds that are represented in phonetic transcription,[1] and to try to carry out all the exercises and suggestions that are given.

Qualifications of the Teacher

(a) Theory and Practice

3. Teachers of French pronunciation should have at least two qualifications: a pronunciation that is French, and the ability to teach it.

4. Some, whose pronunciation is excellent, have had no phonetic training, and find it difficult, if not impossible, to teach their pronunciation to pupils who have passed the imitation stage. Many teachers of French nationality have the same difficulty. It is useless for teachers to assume that the possession of a good pronunciation on their part is all that counts, and that sooner or later their pupils will catch it from them.

5. Others pronounce well and have a considerable knowledge of phonetic theory. But they have no idea

[1] Printed in heavy type.

of using this theory to get good practical results in their teaching.

6. Others have a thorough knowledge of theory side by side with an impossible pronunciation. Their theory, learned without any real association with the spoken language, has left them with the bad pronunciation they always had, and is probably responsible for worse pronunciations in their pupils. It is difficult to help such teachers.

7. Some, alas, have neither the good pronunciation nor the knowledge of phonetics, and are even guilty of making bad worse by using phonetic symbols and charts and diagrams and pocket mirrors and all the rest of the paraphernalia, imagining that by so doing they are teaching by phonetic methods !

8. It is essential that the teacher should learn a certain amount of phonetic theory if he wants his pupils to overcome the difficulties of the pronunciation stage as quickly as possible. What theory is necessary is given here. It should be studied, not as a thing apart, but as the writer has attempted to present it—in relation to its practical application. Many exercises will be suggested by which the reader may improve his own pronunciation, and many hints will be given as to how he can teach the sounds to beginners and correct the sounds of those who make them wrongly.

9. Where helpful, French sounds are compared and contrasted with English ones. The teacher who is aware of English tendencies and can demonstrate them is in a much better position to help his pupils to produce the correct sounds than one who relies solely on his knowledge of the formation of French sounds.

(b) A Good Ear

10. It is impossible to exaggerate the importance of a good ear, without which the learning and teaching

of a spoken language cannot be undertaken with any measure of success. The learner whose ear is closed to the differences between sounds cannot expect to make those differences. The teacher cannot analyse and correct the faults of his pupils if he is deaf to those faults.

11. The necessary training cannot be given by a book. If possible, the teacher whose ear needs training should place himself under the guidance of a trained phonetician who will, by systematic exercises, develop in him the ability to hear so that he can detect even delicate shades of difference between sounds.

12. If trained guidance is impossible, the reader can do much, if he has any aptitude at all, to teach himself to listen carefully to his own English sounds and to try to record them by means of a phonetic transcription ; to note the differences and similarities between his own sounds and those of his friends and acquaintances ; to appreciate the differences between his own vowels and those of French—differences such as those which exist between the ɪ of *mill* and the i of *mille*, the eɪ of *day* and the e of *dé*, the æ of *pat* and the a of *patte*, the ɒ of *not* and the ɔ of *note*, the oʊ of *toe* and the o of *tôt*, the ɜ of *purr* and the ø of *peu*, the ɒŋ of *long* and the ɑ̃ of *lent*.[1] All words under investigation should be pronounced aloud many times, the speaker concentrating on their *sounds*, trying to free himself from the distracting influence of their conventional spelling.

Ear-training for the Pupil

13. Every opportunity should be taken at the outset to make learners accurate listeners. Those teachers who can pronounce the sounds of French well should

---

[1] The phonetic symbols are those of the International Phonetic Association. Most teachers of French are familiar with them. The writer offers no apology for introducing a number of them here, since in each case a key-word is given. A complete list of symbols for English and French sounds is given in Chapter III.

give ear-training exercises to their pupils. Such exercises should be given *before* pupils are required to *make* the sounds, and should be continued in a different form throughout the course.

14. The following method could be adopted. The teacher should pronounce three or four of the French vowel sounds many times. First the vowel of *lit*, *cygne* : i, i, i, i. This sound should then be associated with the symbol i which is written on the board, and numbered 1. Then the vowel of *thé*, *gai*, *pied* : e, e, e, e. This sound should be associated with the symbol e, and numbered 2. Similarly with the vowel of *paix* : ɛ, ɛ, ɛ, ɛ, numbered 3 ; of *patte* : a, a, a, a, numbered 4.

15. These four vowels should then be repeated over and over again by the teacher, sometimes in alternation : i, e, i, e ; e, ɛ, e, ɛ ; ɛ, a, ɛ, a ; sometimes in a different order : ɛ, e, i ; a, ɛ, e ; e, ɛ, i ; a, e, a ; a, e, ɛ ; e, i, e ; i, a, i ; i, e, ɛ, a ; a, ɛ, e, i. This repetition should be done on a monotone, so that the class is not called upon to listen to change of pitch as well as to change of vowel quality. Then, to test the ability of the class to distinguish the vowels readily, the teacher should pronounce them in any order, the pupils writing down the phonetic symbol for the sound they hear, or giving its number. When mistakes are made, the pupils should have the opportunity of hearing the wrong and the right sound over and over again until they can hear the difference.

16. In the same way, the teacher should introduce the vowel sound of *bas* : ɑ, ɑ, ɑ, ɑ, number 5 ; of *pomme* : ɔ, ɔ, ɔ, ɔ, number 6 ; of *beau* : o, o, o, o, number 7 ; of *boue* : u, u, u, u, number 8. The ability of the class to distinguish vowels 1–8 should then be tested.

17. The remaining vowels should be gradually introduced in the same way : y of *lu*, 9 ; ø of *peu*, 10 ;

œ of *œuf*, 11 ; ə of *me*, 12 ; ɛ̃ of *pain*, 13 ; ã of *banc*, 14 ; ɔ̃ of *bon*, 15 ; œ̃ of *brun*, 16.

18. When the pupils can readily hear the difference between e and ɛ, u and y, ø and œ, ã and ɔ̃, œ̃ and ɛ̃, and can, without any hesitation, connect each vowel sound with its appropriate symbol (or number), groups of one syllable containing an easy consonant sound could then be dictated [1] : lu (8), ly (9), pɛ (3), te (2), la (4), ɔm (6), mɔ̃ (15), mo (7), œf (11), tɛ̃ (13), bã (14), etc. Then two or more syllables : l ekɔl, la klɑːs, la krɛ, l elɛːv, lə bã, la mɛ̃, lə tablo, lez ãfã, lə frɑsɛ, etc. Then easy sentences : ʒə m apɛl ʒã, ʒ e ɔ̃z ã, vwasi œ̃ bã, vwala œ̃ liːvr, ki ɛ la? kɔmã vuz aple vu? uvre la pɔrt, etc.

19. From time to time the pupils might be required to listen to a very short, simple story in French, so that their ear may become accustomed to the sounds and the melody of connected speech.

20. As the class progresses and becomes too familiar with real French words, their meaning and their phonetic dress, meaningless words, consisting of French sounds, with here and there an English sound for contrast, can be dictated occasionally, e.g. mitofɛ, sybãe, kalønɔf, udyʒɛ̃, t̠œfɔ̃bɛn, ʒetalœ̃ki, etc.

21. Ear-training exercises are not a waste of time : they have a remarkably stimulating effect on the class, manifested in a general alertness and in an increasing ability to hear and to make the sounds well. They also prepare pupils to grasp quickly what is said to them in French.

22. In the early stages, much can be done, without giving formal lessons, to open the ears of pupils to the intonation of French. The teacher's intonation should, of course, be at least passable. Good gramophone

---

[1] Incidentally, the method of representing each consonant sound is taught.

records are useful throughout the course in providing models of intonation for the class. The teacher can train himself to raise and lower the sound-box while the disc is revolving, so that the intonation of a sentence or of any part of it can be repeated any number of times. This can be done, after a little practice, without damaging the record.

23. After listening many times to the intonation of a word or of a short sentence, most pupils will have no difficulty in realizing the direction of the voice; and the slow ones will be helped if the teacher quickly indicates the intonation pattern by some simple system of marking :—

or, more simply

or

or

according to the type of sentence.[1]

24. The language teacher's life is a hard one, but he will find it easier and much more pleasant if he regards intonation from the outset as an essential characteristic of the spoken language and expects his pupils to do the same. French intonation is made easier to the English pupil if, in the early stages, he is taught simple facts about French stress. It should not be difficult to teach beginners to pronounce unemphatic words, phrases and short sentences with a fairly strong stress

[1] See Chapter XVII.

on the *final* syllable and with regular, even, medium stress on all other syllables, e.g. *le profes'seur*, with the

"tune"

lə prɔ fɛ 'sœːr, and not *le pro'fesseur*,

with English stress and tune ; *les*

ani'maux, with the tune

lez a ni 'mo, and not *les*

'animaux, with English stress and tune

Correct stress and intonation should not be treated as an "extra", to be required only from advanced pupils ; nor ignored altogether as if unnecessary or impossible of attainment.

CHAPTER II

USE AND ABUSE
OF PHONETIC TRANSCRIPTION

25. Can a good pronunciation of French be taught without the use of a phonetic transcription? It has often been done. If the teacher has a good pronunciation and knows how to teach it ; if, too, he is blessed with a good ear, he can, and often does, succeed without the help of a phonetic transcription. But in the opinion of many experienced teachers, he ignores a valuable help.

26. Does a good pronunciation necessarily follow the use of a phonetic transcription? By no means. In the hands of those teachers who think that their whole duty towards pronunciation is done when they have provided their pupils with a list of symbols and the opportunity of reading phonetic texts, a phonetic transcription is nothing but a waste of time.

27. Whether a phonetic transcription is used or not, the pupil must learn the sounds ; and it is the teacher who must teach them. Phonetic symbols have not the magic power to do that.

28. The use of phonetic symbols comes *after* the sounds have been taught. At a time when the pupil is concerned with the difficulties of pronunciation, it is a great convenience if each essential sound can be represented by one letter and not by half a dozen or more ; and if each letter is made to represent one sound, and one only.

29. French spelling represents the pronunciation of French much better than English spelling represents the pronunciation of English ; but it is far from being entirely phonetic. Often one sound is spelt in many

ways. The sound ɛ, for example, is spelt with the letter *e* in *sel* sɛl, *ê* in *bête* bɛːt, *è* in *père* pɛːr, *é* in *donné-je?* dɔnɛːʒ?, *ai* in *laid* lɛ, *ei* in *reine* rɛːn, etc. The sound ɛ̃ is spelt *en* in *rien* rjɛ̃, *in* in *instant* ɛ̃stɑ̃ (but not in *inutile* inytil), *im* in *impossible* ɛ̃pɔsibl (but not in *imitation* imitasjɔ̃), *ein* in *teint* tɛ̃, *ing* in *poing* pwɛ̃, *ain* in *bain* bɛ̃, *aim* in *faim* fɛ̃. Often one letter represents many sounds. The letter *e*, for example, is pronounced ɛ in *sel* sɛl, ə and e in *peser* pəze, a in *femme* fam. It is not pronounced at all in *plume* plym. The letter *c* is pronounced k in *lac* lak, g in *second* səgɔ̃, s in *cent* sɑ̃. The reader will recall many other examples of inconsistency.

30. A phonetic spelling is, above all, a consistent one. With it there is no question of ambiguity and therefore no cause for hesitation. When the pupil has learned each sound and has closely associated each sound with one definite symbol, he has only to look at a word written in phonetic script and he can say it, for its pronunciation is written on its face. With a phonetic transcription a pupil can therefore make much more rapid progress in pronunciation than if he has at the same time to grapple with the difficulties of orthography.

31. Phonetic transcription also acts as a safeguard against the pupil's tendency to import his own sounds into the new language. When he is learning to make the new sounds, each symbol is associated with certain definite instructions and with a certain acoustic result, so that later the mere sight of a symbol should be quite sufficient to remind him of the quality of the sound it represents and of what he must do to produce it.

32. Many teachers have told the writer that they use a phonetic transcription *side by side* with the traditional spelling, with very successful results. This method avoids a transition, it is true ; but conventional orthography at this stage must neutralize the advantages

of a phonetic transcription ; and the burden of carrying two alphabets at once must hamper the pupil's progress, so that the time saved by avoiding a transition stage is only imaginary.

33. A phonetic transcription has other advantages over conventional orthography in that it records, in a clear and easily remembered way, the usage in regard to elision forms, liaison forms, assimilation, length and stress ; whereas the traditional spelling gives, for the most part, no indication at all of these important phenomena.

34. Does it matter *what* phonetic transcription is used? Many teachers, who object to what they consider the waste of time spent on the transition period, prefer a transcription which interferes as little as possible with the conventional spelling. The great disadvantage of such a transcription is that it involves the use of many tiny diacritical marks, italicized letters, etc., which are tiring and bad for the eyesight.

35. If a phonetic transcription is used at all, it is better that it should be bold enough to necessitate a transition period. There are many phonetic alphabets in existence, and it is desirable, in making a choice, to consider the importance of unity as well as of efficacy. The most widely used alphabet is that of the International Phonetic Association. This alphabet does not claim to be perfect. But it has stood the test of forty years, and is now used in hundreds of publications dealing with pronunciation—readers, text-books, dictionaries, etc.

36. How long should a phonetic transcription be used? If circumstances allow, it should be used until the difficulties of pronunciation have been overcome. The amount of time one can actually devote to its use depends largely on the length and aim of the course and the amount of time a week given to French. In a four years' course it would be hardly worth while to

spend less than one term ; though the writer has known of schools in which seven or eight weeks only were allowed, with quite successful results. In a longer course phonetic transcription should be used for a longer period, varying from six months to the ideal period of one year.

37. The work during the phonetic transcription period should, if possible, be all oral : pupils need not be required to *write* phonetic transcription except during ear-training practice, which cannot be given with much success after the very early stages without the use of phonetic symbols.

38. The difficulties of the transition stage have often been greatly exaggerated. If pupils are put on to the right track they will do much of the work of this stage themselves, and enjoy it. They find the whole operation very interesting, for they are always making important discoveries.

39. By the time the transition stage has been reached pupils should know by heart a number of short lessons written phonetically. If they are suddenly introduced to the same lessons in conventional orthography they find the change very bewildering. The attention of the class should therefore be limited, for a time, to the first lesson only, or to some simple rhyme they have memorized, or to the names of things in the classroom. The vowel sounds should be taken in turn, the class giving as many words as they can in which each sound is used. These are written on the blackboard, and at the side of each the conventional spelling, e.g.

ε

fənɛ:tr	fenêtre
la krɛ	la cr*aie*
il ɛ	il *est*
l elɛ:v	l'él*è*ve
la ʃɛ:z	la ch*ai*se

ā

ʒā	Jean
grā	grand
l ãfā	l'enfant
lə tā	le temps
la ʃāːbr	la chambre

The pupils make a copy, underlining the different orthographical forms, and learn the words. Space is left for the addition of examples to each list. Incidentally the pupils learn how the consonant sounds are represented in ordinary spelling.

40. The lessons previously read in phonetic transcription can now be studied in their ordinary spelling. This forms a useful revision period.

41. The objection that phonetic transcription leads to bad spelling has little foundation. The conventional spelling of a word is often such a surprise to a pupil that he remembers it without any difficulty. If the transition stage is effected methodically a very sure grasp of French orthography should follow.

42. After the transition many teachers who have expended on early lessons in pronunciation great energy and enthusiasm tend to lose interest and to tolerate all kinds of slackness. It is surely important that the attempt they have made to set up a good standard of pronunciation should be maintained throughout the course. Systematic practice of the vowel sounds and the more difficult consonants should never be dropped. Frequent exercises should be given for the control of the muscles of the lips and cheeks. Ear-training exercises should be continued and, as the course proceeds, more and more use should be made of the dictation of meaningless words. Frequent reference should be made to the phonetic alphabet in correcting mispronunciations (see § 31). From time to time the class should have practice in the reading of continuous phonetic texts. Even five minutes of each lesson devoted methodically to some form of pronunciation exercise will work wonders.

CHAPTER III

PHONETIC SYMBOLS FOR ENGLISH AND FRENCH SOUNDS

43. Throughout this book the symbols of the International Phonetic Association are used.

A. Symbols for English Sounds

44. The following symbols represent the English vowel and consonant sounds of an educated speaker with a normal pronunciation.

I. Vowel Symbols—English contains both pure vowels [1] and diphthongs.[2]

(a) PURE VOWELS

Symbol		Key-word	Symbol		Key-word
1. i	.	e*a*t	7. ɔ	.	*awe*
2. ɪ	.	*i*t	8. ʊ	.	hood
3. ɛ	.	*e*gg	9. u	.	mood
4. æ	.	m*a*n	10. ʌ	.	d*u*mb
5. ɑ	.	h*a*lf	11. ɜ	.	hear*d*
6. ɒ	.	h*o*t	12. ə	.	sof*a*

(b) DIPHTHONGS

13. eɪ	.	*a*ge	18. ɪə	.	p*ier*
14. oʊ	.	*o*ld	19. ɛə	.	p*ear*
15. aɪ	.	*I*	20. ɔə	.	p*our*
16. aʊ	.	*ou*t	21. ʊə	.	p*oor*
17. ɔɪ	.	*oi*l			

[1] A *pure* vowel is one in which the organs of speech remain stationary for the entire sound. It is represented by one symbol.

[2] A *diphthong* is a vowel sound in which the organs of speech concerned glide from one position to another, the glide being made in such a way that the impression of *one* syllable is given. Diphthongs are represented by two symbols.

II. Consonant Symbols

Symbol		Key-word	Symbol		Key-word
p	.	*p*ark	f	.	*f*at
b	.	*b*ar	v	.	*v*ent
t	.	*t*ar	θ	.	*th*ick
d	.	*d*ark	ð	.	*th*is
k	.	*c*ar	s	.	*s*ee
g	.	*g*uard	z	.	*z*eal
ʧ	.	*ch*eap	ʃ	.	*sh*are
ʤ	.	*j*am	ʒ	.	mea*s*ure
m	.	*m*e	r (ɹ)	.	*r*ed
n	.	*n*o	h	.	*h*at
ŋ	.	ba*ng*	w	.	*w*ise
l	.	*l*eave	j	.	*y*es
ł	.	tab*l*e			

B. Symbols for French Sounds

45. The following symbols represent the sounds used by an educated French speaker.

I. Vowel Symbols—French contains pure vowels only.[1]

	Symbol		Key-word		Symbol		Key-word
1.	i	.	v*i*ve	9.	y	.	m*u*r
2.	e	.	th*é*	10.	ø	.	*eu*x
3.	ε	.	*ai*se	11.	œ	.	s*eu*l
4.	a	.	t*a*ble	12.	ə	.	p*e*ser
5.	ɑ	.	*â*me	13.	ɛ̃	.	b*ain*
6.	ɔ	.	h*o*mme	•14.	ɑ̃	.	b*anc*
7.	o	.	t*ô*t	•15.	ɔ̃	.	b*on*
✗ 8.	u	.	b*ou*e	16.	œ̃	.	br*un*

II. Consonant Symbols

p	.	*p*aix	r ⎫		
b	.	*b*as	ʀ ⎬	.	*r*are
t	.	*t*out	ʁ ⎭		

---

[1] Diphthongs sometimes occur in quick speech, but their use may be disregarded by the foreign learner.

Symbol	Key-word	Symbol	Key-word
d .	*d*os	f .	*f*aux
k .	*c*as	v .	*v*i*v*e
g .	*g*ai	s .	*s*i
m .	*m*ais	z .	*z*éro
n .	*n*on	ʃ .	*ch*anter
ɟ ɲ .	ga*gn*er	ʒ .	*j*upe
l .	*l*ivre	w .	*ou*i
		ɟ ɥ .	h*u*it
		j .	*j*eux

46. *Length* is indicated by : placed after the sound which is lengthened, e.g. mɔ̃ːd *monde*, pɛːr *père*, ‖sːi œrø *si heureux*. As the book is for the use of English readers, length of English sounds is not marked except where it is useful to mark it for purposes of comparison.

47. *Unemphatic stress* is indicated by ' placed before the syllable pronounced with stress.

48. *Emphasis* is indicated by ‖ when the emphasis is for intensity ; by ⫽ when the emphasis is for contrast.

49. *Other symbols and diacritical marks :*

ü, centralized u (see § 159).

c, palatal voiceless plosive (see § 250).

ɟ, palatal voiced plosive (see § 250).

₀ under or over a symbol indicates that the sound represented (usually voiced in the language) is voiceless : pœpl̥ *peuple*, katr̥ *quatre*.

   under or over a symbol indicates that the sound represented (usually voiceless in the language) is voiced : ã faṣ də nu *en face de nous*.

CHAPTER IV

THE ORGANS OF SPEECH

50. The average person is ignorant of the nature of the simplest speech actions he performs every day in pronouncing his own language. There is, of course, no reason why he should study these actions or even be aware that he makes them. But the language teacher should make it his duty to observe his own speech habits closely so that he may the better understand, make and teach those of the speaker of another language. As a necessary preliminary he should have some elementary knowledge of his speech apparatus and of how it works.

51. For the great majority of speech sounds there must be a stream of air set in motion by lung pressure. The passage through which this reaches the outer air is constantly changing its shape, these changes being brought about by the different positions many of our organs of speech can assume.

52. The diagram on p. 17 illustrates the organs of speech. If you turn your back to a strong light and let a mirror reflect this light into your mouth, you can see in comfort most of these organs for yourself.

53. The roof of the mouth is divided into three parts. (Feel them with the tip of your tongue.) Behind the upper teeth is the *teeth-ridge*. Behind that is the *hard palate*, which stretches back to a point where the roof of the mouth begins to feel soft and flabby. There the *soft palate*, sometimes called the velum, begins. This is the only movable part of the roof of the mouth. Hanging from the extreme end of the soft palate is the uvula. This is capable of a movement independent

of that of the soft palate as a whole, a movement necessary in articulating a uvular rolled *r*.

54. In order to make as clear as possible descriptions of the formation of sounds it is convenient to divide the tongue also into three parts : the *blade*, including

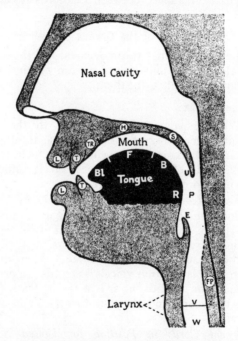

DIAGRAM 1—THE ORGANS OF SPEECH.

B, Back of Tongue ; Bl, Blade of Tongue ; E, Epiglottis ; F, Front of Tongue ; FP, Food Passage ; H, Hard Palate ; LL, Lips ; P, Pharyngal Cavity (Pharynx) ; R, Root of Tongue ; S, Soft Palate ; TT, Teeth ; TR, Teeth-ridge ; U, Uvula ; V, Position of Vocal Cords ; W, Windpipe.

its extremity, the tip ; the *front*, lying beneath the hard palate ; the *back* lying beneath the soft palate. All these parts of the tongue are capable of movement. So also are the lower jaw and the lips.

55. The *pharynx* is the space in the throat just behind the mouth.

56. In the upper part of the windpipe is the *larynx*, in which are the vocal cords or vocal lips. These consist of two folds of membrane stretching horizontally across the larynx. The space between the cords is called the *glottis*.

Movements of the Organs of Speech

57. Let us see what the movements of these organs of speech can be, and how a stream of air from the lungs can be modified by them.

1. In the Larynx

58. What movements are possible in the larynx? It is quite unnecessary for our purpose to attempt to understand the complex mechanism which regulates the movements of the vocal cords. It is sufficient to know what those movements are.

59. *Vocal Cords in Position for Voiceless Sounds*— Sometimes the vocal cords are wide apart, so that when the air-stream passes through it meets with very little opposition here ; it brushes gently against their edges, but without causing them to vibrate. When the vocal cords are in this position voiceless sounds are produced. Pronounce the sounds h, s, f, θ (as in *thin*), ʃ (as in *share*) with your hand on your throat. You will feel no vibration.

60. *Vocal Cords in Position for Voiced Sounds*— Sometimes the vocal cords are drawn together and held loosely, so that the air-stream has to force its way through. It does this in a succession of extremely rapid little puffs or vibrations, the action producing a sound having musical pitch, i.e. *voice*. The pitch varies according to the rapidity of the vibrations : the more rapid they are, the higher the pitch. Any sound accompanied by this vibration is called a voiced sound. Pronounce the vowel of *alms*, *eat*, *all*, the z of *buzz*,

the ʒ of *measure*, the sounds m, n. With your fingers on
your throat you will readily become conscious of the
vibration of the vocal cords, i.e. of voice.

61. Pronounce again the sound z, feeling the
vibration. Now pronounce s. The articulation is the
same. But for s the vocal cords do not vibrate.
Pronounce ʒ and ʃ. They have the same articulation.
The difference is due to a difference in the position of
the vocal cords. ʒ is accompanied by a musical note ;
ʃ is not. Pass from a prolonged z to a prolonged s
without a break between the two sounds. You will
then have the sensation of passing from a voiced sound
to a voiceless one.

62. All sounds either are or are not accompanied by
voice. Each voiced sound has a voiceless counterpart.
Can you make an *m* which has no voice? First make the
voiced sound. Then, with your lips still together, let
the air pass through your nose without the accompaniment of voice. The air will pass through the nose
in greater volume than for voiced *m*, since it is not
held back in the larynx to set the vocal cords in vibration.
Can you make a voiceless rolled *r*? a voiceless *l*?
a voiceless i? Voiceless *m* is occasionally heard in
French, and voiceless *r* and *l* very frequently. i, y and
u are often pronounced without voice when the syllables
in which they occur have a very low pitch.

63. Voiceless sounds in common use have a special
symbol, e.g. θ, f, s, ʃ, p, t, k. Voiceless sounds which
do not often occur in languages have no special symbol
assigned to them. A tiny ring, suggestive of the open
position of the vocal cords, is placed beneath the symbol
used for the voiced counterpart, or above the symbol
in the case of tailed letters, e.g. m̥, r̥, l̥, i̥, ẙ.

64. It is the voiced sounds which carry the tune when
we speak and when we sing. You will find that it is
possible to sing up the scale on the sound z or ʒ, but
impossible on s or ʃ.

65. Knowledge of the difference between voiced sounds and voiceless ones helps the learner to understand and to make the difference between the voiced plosives and fricatives of French and those of English. This knowledge is also necessary to understand the process of assimilation.

66. *Vocal Cords in the Position of the Glottal Stop*— There are less important movements of the vocal cords, one of which should be noticed. We can bring the vocal cords quite close together and suddenly part them. The result is a complete silence followed by a puff of air, the whole resembling a weak cough. This sound is called the glottal plosive, the symbol for which is ˀ.

67. ˀ is a sound just as much as p, which it resembles, is a sound ; and it has a distinct effect in speech. If it occurs immediately before a vowel sound it gives a sudden beginning to that sound : ˀɑ, ˀi, ˀɛ ; immediately after, it brings the vowel sound to an abrupt close : ɑˀ, iˀ, ɛˀ ; between vowels it has the effect of marking syllable division very sharply : ɑˀɑˀɑ, ɛˀɛˀɛ. Before a consonant the sound consists only of the silence : no plosion is heard, e.g. nɒˀ bæd, kæˀtʃ—pronunciations commonly heard from English people instead of nɒt bæd *not bad*, kætʃ *catch*.

68. The glottal plosive is an essential consonant sound in many languages, e.g. in Danish, Arabic, in many Chinese and African languages. It is very frequently heard in German. The sound occurs in English, though it is never essential. We use it, for example, when we want to emphasize a syllable beginning with a vowel : wɒt ɒn ‖ˀɜθ ɑ ju ˈduɪŋ? *What on earth are you doing?* hi z ən ‖ˀæbsəlut ˈfeɪljə *he's an absolute failure*.

69. ˀ is becoming more and more common in other positions in the speech of English people. Listen to yourself and try to find out if you say mɪstə ˀætkɪnz or mɪstər ætkɪnz *Mr. Atkins*, dʒæfə ˀɒrɪndʒ or dʒæfə

ɒrɪndʒ *Jaffa orange*,[1] kɒˀn or kɒtn *cotton*, kæˀtʃ or kætʃ *catch*, nɒˀ bæd or nɒt bæd *not bad*.[2]

70. English people who may use the glottal stop very sparingly while speaking their own language are often tempted to pronounce it frequently in French, especially when reading or speaking with an effort. Their tendency is to use it as the initial sound of many words which should begin with a vowel. The glottal stop is very distasteful to French people. There *are* French speakers who use it in emphasis, but it is never necessary, and English learners would do well to avoid it altogether.

The above are the chief positions the vocal cords may assume.

2. In the Mouth

71. The air-stream is still further modified in the mouth which changes shape according to the position of the various movable organs there, thus making a great number of speech sounds possible.

(*a*) *The Lips*

72. The lips can be bunched up and pushed forward in a most un-English fashion, lengthening out the mouth cavity. They can be drawn tightly across the teeth, with corners far apart. They can be placed in positions intermediate between these. Each change of position affects the sound made.

73. Try to pronounce in isolation an English vowel which is made with no protrusion of the lips, e.g. the i of *eat* or the ɛ of *egg*. Then, still aiming at the quality

---

[1] Perhaps you say dʒæfər ɒrɪndʒ!

[2] Readers are probably aware that ˀ is a common sound in many English and Scottish dialects, where it often replaces t, and less often p and k in certain positions. In these dialects *letter* is pronounced lɛˀə, *Saturday* sæˀədɪ, *particle* pɑˀɪkl, *dirty* dɜˀɪ, *chocolate* tʃɒˀlɪˀ, *shopman* ʃɒˀmən.

of i or of ɛ, use strong lip-rounding. Note the different vowel produced. Try to make in isolation an English rounded vowel, e.g. the u of *rule*. Now aim at the same u-sound with the corners of the lips stretched far apart. (This is not easy to do.) Note the change of quality. Try with other vowels the experiment of completely changing the lip position. Lip position is important, especially to English learners of French. Reference will often be made to it later, in the descriptions of French vowel sounds.

(b) The Tongue

74. The tongue is not always placed as shown in Diagram 1. Its various parts can assume different positions. At present these will be described very briefly.

75. The *tip* can be placed almost between the teeth as for the θ of *thin* and the ð of *then* ; t, d, n, l can be articulated in the same place (dental). The tip or blade can be raised to different parts of the teeth-ridge for another variety (alveolar) of t, d, n, l ; also for s, z, r, ʃ, ʒ. The tip can be curled back to touch the hard palate where still another variety (retroflex) of t, d, n, l can be made. It is also possible to make a retroflex r, s, z, ʃ, ʒ.

76. The *front* of the tongue can be raised from an almost flat position to a number of higher positions, higher and higher towards the hard palate until the passage through the mouth is closed altogether :—

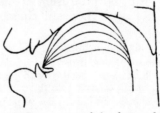

DIAGRAM 2—Movements of the front of the tongue.

77. The *back* is capable of the same kind of movement. We ·can raise it to various heights from the low position necessary for the ɑ of *calm* until the air-passage becomes narrower and narrower and finally disappears :—

DIAGRAM 3—Movements of the back of the tongue.

78. It is also possible to raise that part of the tongue which is intermediate between the front and the back.

(c) The Soft Palate

79. One other important movable organ of speech which can modify the shape of the air-passage is the soft palate. This can be raised, so that the passage through the nasal cavity is closed to the air-stream from the lungs, which must proceed through the mouth :—

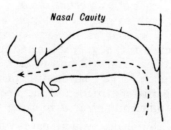

DIAGRAM 4—Soft palate in raised position.

It can be lowered, so that the nasal cavity is opened, allowing the air-stream to pass through. Nasalization depends on this movement of the soft palate :—

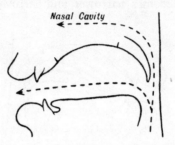

Nasal Cavity

DIAGRAM 5—Soft palate in lowered position.

Vowels and Consonants

80. With this apparatus, just briefly described, we can make an enormous number of speech sounds. These are broadly classified into *vowel* sounds and *consonant* sounds. What is the difference between vowel and consonant? At the root of the difference is what is known as carrying-power.

81. Consonants are produced under conditions of restraint which militate against a high carrying-power. For example, the articulation of p, b, t, d, k, g necessitates a *complete closure* of the mouth-passage for a short time ; that of l a *partial closure* ; f, v, s, z ʃ, ʒ are produced with so great a *narrowing* of the passage that friction is caused as the air squeezes through. Make the sounds f, t, g, ʒ, ʔ, s, l, b and try to describe their articulation. You will find in each case that the sound owes much of its characteristic quality either to complete or partial obstruction of the air-passage or to a narrowing sufficiently great as to cause friction.

82. Those consonants which have voice carry, of course, farther than those without voice.

83. For vowels, the tongue is so held that the passage through the mouth (sometimes *also* the nasal passage) is free, or free enough to allow the air-stream to pass without the accompaniment of friction. Thus, for French i the front of the tongue is raised to what may be called the vowel limit, represented more or less accurately in the following diagram by a dotted line :—

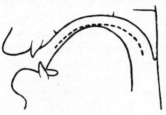

DIAGRAM 6—Tongue position of French vowel i which reaches line of limit for vowel sounds.

If the tongue is raised higher it enters the consonant area where friction is produced :—

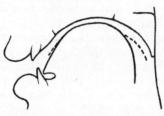

DIAGRAM 7—Tongue position of fricative consonant j which is articulated above the vowel limit.

84. Pronounce the i of *eat*, the ε of *egg*, the æ of *and*, the ɔ of *awe*, the ɜ of *err*. You will not find present the conditions of restraint which characterize consonant sounds.

85. Vowels are voiced sounds.

CHAPTER V

THE CLASSIFICATION OF
VOWELS IN GENERAL

86. It is very important that the teacher of French pronunciation should understand how vowels are classified, for the teaching and correcting of vowel sounds are largely based on a knowledge of their classification. It will be seen later that there are many ways of teaching and correcting French vowel sounds possible to one who understands their formation and their relation to other vowel positions both of English and French.

87. The theory of vowel classification should help the teacher to improve his own pronunciation, but it should on no account be taught to pupils. The sounds of French can be taught to beginners quickly and well without troubling them with phonetic theory. First teach your pupils to *hear* the vowels accurately. Give them the kind of ear-training exercise suggested in Chapter I. When they can readily distinguish the vowels let them have a chance to *imitate* each sound, helping them, if necessary, with simple instructions in regard to those things over which they have some control : the degree of mouth-opening, the strength or weakness of effort required, the position of the lips, of the tip of the tongue. Even these instructions imply a knowledge on the part of the teacher of the formation of the sounds concerned. Pupils have no difficulty in carrying out such simple instructions, especially if they use a pocket-mirror which shows them at once if their lip position and mouth-opening are correct. But if it is a question of wrong *tongue* position a pocket-mirror cannot do the trick. In the case of many vowel sounds,

e.g. y, ø, o, u, it is useless to tell your pupils to look at the tongue position, for it is not visible. It is useless to *talk* about tongue positions or to draw diagrams of tongue positions, for, apart from the tip, pupils have little control over their tongues. It is when imitation has failed, when simple instructions have failed, that the teacher uses his knowledge of the classification of vowels and gives hints which are the outcome of that knowledge.

88. The quality of a vowel sound depends largely on the shape of the cavity through which the air passes, and that shape depends on the position of the movable organs of speech already described.

89. The most important thing which determines the quality of vowels is the position of the tongue, and this is used as the basis for their classification.

Front Vowels

90. Throw your head slightly back and watch the movements of your tongue while you pronounce in succession the a of *patte*, the ε of *aise*, the e of *thé*, the i of *vive*.

91. You should notice two things while making these sounds, even if you do not make them quite accurately : (1), that it is the *front* of the tongue which is raised in each case. (The blade is down, with the tip against the lower teeth.) These vowels are therefore classified as *front*. They are, moreover, true front vowels, for there is no series possible farther forward. (2), that the front is raised to a different height for each vowel.

92. For a the passage left between the tongue and the roof of the mouth is wide. a is therefore called an *open* vowel. (See Diagram 8.)

93. For i the tongue is raised as close to the palate as it can be in producing a vowel. i is therefore called a *close* vowel. (See Diagram 8.)

94. For ε the tongue is raised to approximately a third of the distance between a and i. It may therefore be called *half-open*. (See Diagram 8.)

C

95. For e the tongue is raised to approximately two-thirds of the distance between a and i. It may therefore be called *half-close*. (See Diagram 8.)

96. These vowels i, e, ε, a are, then, classified as *front* according to which part of the tongue is raised ; and as *close*, *half-close*, *half-open* and *open* according to the degree of elevation :—

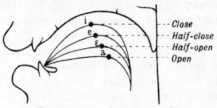

DIAGRAM 8—Front vowels.

97. There are many front vowel positions possible between i and e, between e and ε, between ε and a. In fact, all the front vowels of all the languages of the world are made by raising the front of the tongue to the a-position or to the i-position or to some position intermediate between these two extremes. We have chosen four French vowels to illustrate the principles of vowel classification because they happen to provide good examples of the four degrees of opening and because they are of special interest to us.

Back Vowels

98. Pronounce the ɑ of *âme, pas*, or the vowel of *alms, half*. Alternate this with French a or with English æ of *add*, keeping the tip of the tongue against the lower teeth so that the action of the main part of the tongue may be the better observed. You can *feel* that the raising for ɑ is made by a different part of the tongue than that for a or æ. Look in a mirror and you will notice that for ɑ the front of the tongue is slightly depressed and the back slightly raised. Now try to make an ɑ-sound farther back, as far back as possible.

The sound you make should be similar to the vowel of English *on* but should have a wide-open mouth and no lip-rounding. This is the most retracted back vowel it is possible to make ; and the tongue is in the lowest possible position for a vowel. This position may, for these reasons, be regarded as a cardinal point. We shall compare that of French ɑ with it later.

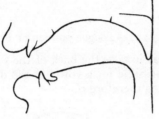

DIAGRAM 9—Tongue position of Cardinal vowel ɑ.

99. Now make the English ɔ of *awe*, *saw*. We have chosen this to illustrate the principles of vowel classification because it is, in the pronunciation of the majority of English speakers, a true back vowel with the tongue raised to approximately one-third of the distance between ɑ and the highest possible back vowel position. It is therefore *half-open*. We shall compare French ɔ with this later.

DIAGRAM 10—Tongue position of English vowel ɔ (*saw*).

100. For o as in *beau* the back of the tongue is raised to approximately two-thirds of the distance between

α and the highest possible back vowel position. It is therefore *half-close* :—

DIAGRAM 11—Tongue position of French o.

101. For u as in *boue* the back of the tongue is raised as high as is possible for a vowel in the direction of the soft palate. It is therefore *close* :—

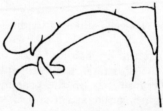

DIAGRAM 12—Tongue position of French u.

102. These vowels : Cardinal α, English ɔ, French o, French u are chosen from a large number of possible vowel positions. They are classified as *back* because the back of the tongue is raised in forming them ; and as *open*, *half-open*, *half-close* and *close* according to the height of raising :—

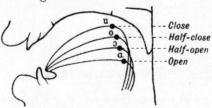

DIAGRAM 13—Back vowels.

103. If the highest points to which the tongue is raised in making these front and back vowels are joined together, a figure of the following queer shape is obtained :—

DIAGRAM 14—The vowel area.

X-ray photographs show this to be the approximate shape of the vowel area. The figure therefore provides a place for recording all possible vowel positions. Those we have at present classified are on the circumference of the figure.

104. This complicated diagram, however, is not convenient to draw every time it is necessary to show the relation between one vowel position and another. It is much simpler and clearer to enclose the vowel area within a straight-lined figure of this kind :—

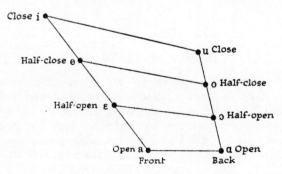

DIAGRAM 15—Simplified diagram of the vowel area.

On the left line are placed true front vowels such as the i, e, ɛ, a we have classified ; on the extreme right line true back vowels such as the ɑ, ɔ, o, u we have classified.

Central Vowels

105. Vowels which are made by raising neither the front nor the back, but an intermediate part of the tongue are called *central*.   Such are the ə of *sofa* ˈsoufə, the ɜ of *early* ˈɜlɪ, the ə of *le* lə, *te* tə, *peser* pəze, the first element of what is often called the " Oxford " pronunciation· of the diphthong of *stone*, the Cockney vowel of *move*.

106. The term central does not include open vowels, i.e. vowels formed with the tongue low down in the mouth.   It includes only those vowels with tongue positions which can be placed in the triangular area shown in the diagram :—

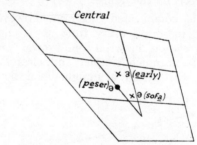

DIAGRAM 16—Central vowels.

107. Some central vowels are often called *neutral*. This term is used in describing those central vowels which have positions in the lower part of the triangular area shown in Diagram 16 and which lack the definite quality that considerable lip-rounding gives, e.g. the ə of *sofa* soufə, the ə of *peser* pəze,[1] the ɜ of *early* ɜlɪ.

---

[1] The ə of *peser* is only slightly rounded.

Unrounded and Rounded Vowels

108. Diagram 15 shows tongue positions only. The lips, as we have seen, play a part; and vowels are also classified according to lip position. i, e, ɛ, a are all *unrounded* to different degrees. More detailed information as to the lip position of these vowels will be given later. For vowels of the ɑ type the corners of the lips are drawn slightly more together than for vowels of the a type, but the lips cannot be said to be rounded. For vowels of the ɔ, o and u types the lips are *rounded* to different degrees. Detailed information as to the degree of rounding necessary for the back vowels occurring in French will be given later.

109. The majority of front vowels occurring in languages are unrounded, and the majority of back vowels rounded. But it is possible to pronounce front vowels with rounded lips and back vowels with unrounded lips. With the latter we are not concerned. With the former we are, since there are three *front rounded* vowels in French : y as in *lune*, ø as in *peu*, œ as in *seul*. More definite information about the tongue and lip positions of these vowels is given later.

Oral and Nasalized Vowels

110. Vowels made with the soft palate in its raised position, so that all the air-stream must pass through the mouth, are called *oral*. Such are all the English vowels, and the French vowels i, e, ɛ, a, ɑ, ɔ, o, u, y, ø, œ, and ə.

111. Since movements of the soft palate are not dependent upon movements of the tongue, all the above vowel positions, and any others, can be held while the soft palate is lowered. Vowels made with the soft palate in its lowered position so that both mouth and nose passages are open to the air-stream are called *nasalized*. In French there are four nasalized vowels : ɛ̃ as in *pain*, ɑ̃ as in *banc*, ɔ̃ as in *non* and œ̃ as in *brun*. The tongue and lip position of these will be discussed later.

Tense and Lax Vowels

112. Tenseness implies a tightening up of the muscles of the tongue, lips, cheeks, probably also of the vocal cords, so that the sound produced is vigorous, clean-cut, the opposite of lax, flabby, slack, indistinct. French vowel positions are more vigorously maintained than English ones, and to know this often helps an English learner to improve his pronunciation of the vowel sounds.

113. Another classification could be made into *wide-pharynxed* and *narrow-pharynxed* vowels. This classification is not of great practical importance. (See, however, § 117, 2 (*b*) (ii).)

CHAPTER VI

THE FRENCH FRONT UNROUNDED VOWELS
i (No. 1)

114. *Words containing* i : *vive* vi:v, *livre* li:vr, *dire* di:r, *bise* bi:z, *public* pyblik, *lit* li, *vif* vif, *abîme* abim, *cygne* siɲ, *comédie* kɔmedi.

115. **Description of i.** (See Diagram 17)

1. The front of the tongue is raised.

2. It is raised to the highest position possible for a vowel. (In the case of some speakers it is slightly lower.) i is therefore a *close* vowel.

3. The lips are spread, i.e. the corners are drawn well apart :

There is little space between the jaws.

4. Muscular effort of the tongue and lips is necessary, giving to the sound a crisp, clean-cut quality.

116. **Comparison with nearest English Sounds**

English learners are tempted in most stressed syllables to substitute the following sounds for French i :—

(a) When i occurs long or finally the tendency (except when r follows) is to use the sound of *eat*, *see*. This vowel is generally different from French i in tongue position, in lip position, and in the amount of muscular effort with which it is produced :—

1. *Tongue Position*—All English people do not use the same vowel in *see*, etc.

Some say si: with a pure vowel which has a lower tongue position than French i. (See (*a*) in Diagram 17.)

Others say sɪi, the tongue starting approximately in the position of English ɪ as in *is* ɪz and moving in the direction of English i. (See (*b*) in Diagram 17.)

Others use a diphthong requiring a still lower position of the tongue for the initial element. This diphthong can be represented by əɪ, though, except in the London and other dialects, the starting point is not so low as it is shown in the diagram. (See (*c*) in Diagram 17.)

2. *Lip Position*—English i, ɪi, əɪ do not require spread lips. The lip position for these sounds is more neutral than spread. If this position is used in attempting French the resulting vowel sounds y-like to French ears.

(*b*) In words like *dire* diːr, *lire* liːr, *pire* piːr, etc. the tendency is to substitute the diphthong of *dear* dɪə, *eer* lɪə, *pier* pɪə, the ə doing duty for r. (See (*d*) in Diagram 17.)

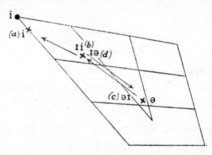

DIAGRAM 17—French i and vowels substituted for it by English learners.

The English tendency, then, is to substitute a sound for which the tongue position is too low and too retracted, and which requires, in the case of the majority of speakers, a movement of the tongue and lower jaw after the sound has begun.

117. **Teaching Hints**

1. *Lip Position*—The lip position is easier to correct than the tongue position. As a rule, it is sufficient if the teacher alternates French i and English i (or ɪi, etc.), drawing attention to the difference in lip position and requiring at first an exaggeration of this difference. (Use mirror.)

2. *Tongue Position*

(*a*) Those who use a pure i in English should be required to spread the lips, put the tip of the tongue against the lower teeth, and use a little more muscular energy. This should give a slightly higher tongue position and a more clean-cut quality to the sound.

(*b*) Those who use a diphthong are more difficult to correct. The teacher should use his knowledge of the tongue position required for French i and for the unsuccessful attempt made. Alternate French i with ɪi (or əɪ), illustrating the difference in lip position and in the position of the lower jaw. When the learner realizes that no jaw movement must accompany his sound he is on the way to success. How can he be helped to use a higher and more advanced tongue position? It is useless to *describe* tongue positions, or to suggest that all he has to do is to raise the tongue higher, for he has not the necessary control to do this. As a general rule, in correcting a wrong tongue position, the teacher should tell the pupil to aim at a vowel which has a tongue position *beyond* the one he is attempting to reach. But there is no vowel beyond French i to aim at. The following methods can be used :

(i) Ask the pupil to try to produce an energetic i *with friction*, i.e. the fricative consonant j. If he can do this, it probably means that the tongue is raised too high. (See Diagram 7.) When the friction has been eliminated the tongue position should be correct.

(ii) It is a good plan to let the pupil watch you do this experiment. Put a finger firmly under the chin near the throat and pronounce English ɪ as in *is*. The finger is not noticeably displaced by muscular action. Then pronounce French i. The finger is displaced considerably by the swelling out of the muscle. (French i requires a wide pharynx.) Invite the pupil, while attempting French i, to try and displace his finger in the same way. After a few trials he will use extra muscular energy to do this, with the result that the front of his tongue will be raised to a greater height.

118. Exercises

The sound i should be practised first very long, without any movement of the tongue or lower jaw. (Use mirror.) Then short. Then in syllables with easy consonants. In teaching, the important points in connection with the easier consonants can be dealt with incidentally.

(*a*) fiː, fi; viː, vi; miː, mi; niː, ni; liː, li; siː, si; fiːf, fif; viːv, viv; miːm, mim; niːn, nin; siːs, sis; fiːv, fiv; fiːm, fim; fiːn, fin; fiːs, fis; viːf, vif; viːm, vim; viːn, vin; viːs, vis; miːf, mif; miːv, miv; miːn, min; miːs, mis; niːf, nif; niːv, niv; niːm, nim; niːs, nis; liːf, lif; liːv, liv; liːm, lim; liːn, lin; liːs, lis.

(*b*) ki *qui*, ki li? *Qui lit?* dis *dix*, di li *dix lits*, sis *six*, si ni *six nids*, midi *midi*, isi *ici*, wi *oui*, ʒə di wi *je dis oui*, si fis *six fils*.

(*c*) Words like *dire* diːr, *pire* piːr, should not be attempted until the difficulty of r has been overcome. They should be practised in two parts diː—r, liː—r, the parts being brought together when both sounds are satisfactory.

(*d*) Words containing the sound l finally, e.g. *mille* mil, and before a consonant, e.g. *il fait* il fɛ,[1] should not be practised until the difficulty of pronouncing l in these positions has been mastered.

---

[1] i fɛ in quick speech.

e (No. 2)

119. *Words containing* e : *thé* te, *assez* ase, *gai* ge, *chanter* ʃɑ̃te, *pied* pje.

120. **Description of e.** (See Diagram 18)

1. The front of the tongue is raised.

2. It is raised to about two-thirds of the distance from the lowest to the highest vowel positions. e is therefore *half-close*.

3. The lips are spread, but the jaws are a little more apart than for i.

4. Muscular effort of the tongue and lips is necessary, giving the sound a crisp, clean-cut quality.

121. **Comparison with nearest English Sounds**

e is a difficult sound for the majority of English learners whose greatest mistake is to substitute for it the diphthong they use in *day* deɪ. This English diphthong varies in character from speaker to speaker, but in all cases it differs from French e in tongue position, in lip position, and in the amount of energy used.

1. *Tongue Position*

(*a*) Some speakers, in pronouncing *day*, start with a vowel considerably lower than French e, the tongue then gliding in the direction of English ɪ : eɪ. (See (*a*) in Diagram 18.)

(*b*) With others, the initial element of the diphthong has a still lower position, similar to that required for the ɛ of *egg* : ɛɪ. (See (*b*) in Diagram 18.)

(*c*) Others, with a distinctly dialectal pronunciation, e.g. Cockneys, many South Midlanders, start with a vowel as open as French ɛ : ɛɪ, or even more open still : æɪ (the æ being generally centralized), or aɪ. (See (*c*) in Diagram 18.)

In all these diphthongs the tongue movement is accompanied by a movement of the lower jaw.

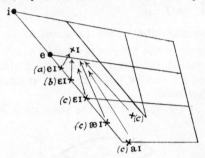

DIAGRAM 18—French e and varieties of eɪ in English *day*.

Thus the English learner tends to say teɪ, tɛɪ, etc., for te *thé*, leɪʒeɪ or lɛɪʒɛɪ, etc., for leʒe *léger*.

2. *Lip Position*—The lip position used in pronouncing the vowel of *day* is generally neutral, the jaws becoming closer as the sound proceeds.

122. Teaching Hints

1. *Lip Position*—The pupil should be required to put the tip of his tongue *firmly* against the lower teeth and spread the lips energetically.

2. *Tongue Position*

(*a*) Alternate English eɪ (or ɛɪ) with French e. This comparison may help the pupil to avoid any movement, i.e. to produce the initial element only of his diphthong. This, as we have seen, is too open. To close it the pupil should try to make it a little like French i, which he has already learned.

(*b*) If the pupil cannot resist the temptation to diphthongize, let him start from French i. In order to get the tongue lower he should make this a little like his sound in *egg*, *without moving his lips*. From time to time the teacher should repeat the correct sound, insisting on the right lip position. This is the best method for class-teaching.

(c) The writer has sometimes found it necessary to get the learner—especially the adult learner who cannot dissociate French e from his diphthong eɪ—to regard French e as a kind of ɪ as in *is*.[1] Isolate this ɪ of *is*, making it long. It is not identical in tongue position with French e, but it is made with the tongue raised to about the same height (see Diagram 18) ; and it has the advantage, as a starting point, of being a pure vowel. (If you can alternate English ɪ with French e you will perhaps realize that ɪ is pronounced laxly, and is not a true front vowel.) How can the learner make a sound farther forward and introduce into it the necessary clean-cut quality ? Try for yourself to carry out the following instructions :—

(i) Spread the lips so that the corners are far apart.

(ii) Put the tip of your tongue firmly against the lower teeth.

(iii) Aim at an *energetic* ɪ.

The result should be a good French e.

123. Exercises

The sound e needs a great deal of practice. It should be practised very long, with no movement of the organs of speech after it has started. (Use mirror.) Then short. Then in combination with easy consonants :—

(a) feː, fe ; veː, ve ; meː, me ; neː, ne ; leː, le ; seː, se ; feːf, fef ; veːv, vev ; meːm, mem ; neːn, nen ; seːs, ses ; feːv, fev ; veːf, vef ; veːm, vem ; veːn, ven ; veːs, ves ; meːf, mef ; meːv, mev ; meːn, men ; meːs, mes ; neːf, nef ; neːv, nev ; neːm, nem ; neːs, nes ; leːf, lef ; leːv, lev ; leːm, lem ; leːn, len ; leːs, les.

(b) le ni *les nids*, le fe *les fées*, le site *les cités*, lize *lisez*, le de *les dés*, l epe *l'épée*, le ne *les nez*, l ete *l'été*, le bebe *les bébés*, le fis *les fils*, lə dine *le dîner*, lə ke *le quai*, vizite *visiter*, le lise *les lycées*, ʃe ki *Chez qui?*

---

[1] It is not safe to suggest that French e is like the ɪ of *heavy* ˈhɛvɪ, for some English speakers diphthongize ɪ when it is quite final ; others use too open a sound.

ɛ (No. 3)

124. *Words containing* ɛ : *bête* bɛːt, *treize* trɛːz, *crême* krɛːm, *ai-je?* ɛːʒ? *fier* fjɛːr, *verre* vɛːr, *père* pɛːr, *sèche* sɛʃ, *siècle* sjɛkl̩.

125. **Description of** ɛ. (See Diagram 19)

1. The front of the tongue is raised.

2. It is raised to about one-third of the distance between the lowest and highest vowel positions. ɛ is therefore *half-open*.

3. The corners of the lips are drawn apart. The mouth-opening is greater than for e.

126. **Comparison with nearest English Sounds**

The sounds substituted for ɛ by English speakers vary according to position.

(*a*) When the sound occurs short in a closed syllable,[1] as in *peine* pɛn, the tendency is to use the vowel of English *pen* pɛn which is usually too close. (See (*a*) in Diagram 19.)

(*b*) When the sound occurs in an open syllable,[2] as in *aimer* ɛme, *très* trɛ, the tendency is to substitute the diphthong of *day* deɪ. (See (*b*) in Diagram 19, which shows one variety of this diphthong.) There is the same tendency when the sound occurs long, as in *treize* trɛːz, which the English learner wants to pronounce in the same way as *trays* treɪz. (See (*b*) in Diagram 19.)

(*c*) When ɛ is followed by the sound r, as in *père* pɛːr, *affaire* afɛːr, *perte* pɛrt, the English learner's tendency is to use the diphthong he has in *pear* pɛə, *affair* əfɛə. (See (*c*) in Diagram 19.)

---

[1] A closed syllable is one ending in a consonant sound, e.g. *peine* pɛn, *sept* sɛt.

[2] An open syllable is one ending in a vowel sound, e.g. *très* trɛ, *lait* lɛ.

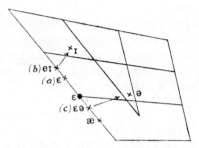

DIAGRAM 19—French ɛ and vowels substituted for it by English learners.

127. Teaching Hints

1. Insist on the correct mouth opening and lip position. The tip of the tongue should touch the lower teeth.

2. *Tongue Position*

(*a*) Those who use pure ɛ as in *pen*, *egg*, which is too close for French ɛ, should *open the mouth wider*. This may lead to a corresponding lowering of the tongue. If it does not, the learner should aim at making his sound a little æ-like. æ has a lower tongue position than is required. (See Diagram 19.)

(*b*) The learner who substitutes the English diphthong eɪ should start from French e, which he has already learned. A good French ɛ may be obtained from this by opening the mouth wider and by modifying the sound in the direction of English æ.

(*c*) The use of ɛə for French ɛ is more difficult to avoid. The fact that the learner can pronounce French ɛ in isolation does not necessarily mean that he can pronounce words like *père*, *mère*, *chère*. These words can be practised only when the difficulty of r has been overcome. They should be pronounced in two parts, pɛː—r, mɛː—r, etc., the two parts being brought together when both sounds are satisfactory.

D

128. **Exercises**

The sound ε should be practised both long and short, first in isolation, then in easy groups :—

(a) fεː, fε ; vεː, vε ; mεː, mε ; nεː, nε ; lεː, lε ; sεː, sε ; fεːf, fεf ; vεːv, vεv ; mεːm, mεm ; nεːn, nεn ; sεːs, sεs ; fεːv, fεv ; fεːm, fεm ; fεːn, fεn ; fεːs, fεs ; vεːf, vεf ; vεːm, vεm ; vεːn, vεn ; vεːs, vεs ; mεːf, mεf ; mεːv, mεv ; mεːn, mεn ; mεːs, mεs ; nεːf, nεf ; nεːv, nεv ; nεːm, nεm ; nεːs, nεs ; lεːf, lεf ; lεːv, lεv ; lεːm, lεm ; lεːn, lεn ; lεːs, lεs.

(b) l elεːv *l'élève*, elεn *Hélène*, il ε·il est, il εt isi *il est ici*, fεːt *fête*, bεːt *bête*, il fε *il fait*, εde *aider*, sεt *sept*, sεt elεːv *sept élèves*, siz elεːv *six élèves*, sεːz *seize*, sεz elεːv *seize élèves*, pεje *payer*, k ε s kə s ε? *Qu'est-ce que c'est?*

a (No. 4)

129. *Words containing* a : *part* paːr, *soir* swaːr, *quart* kaːr, *sage* saːʒ, *table* tabl, *chasser* ʃase, *donnâmes* dɔnam, *soif* swaf.

130. **Description of a.** (See Diagram 20)

1. The front of the tongue is raised.

2. The raising is very slight. a is therefore an *open* vowel.

3. The mouth is more open than for ε, the corners of the lips drawn apart.

131. **Comparison with nearest English Sounds**

The sound a is difficult for southern English learners who substitute for it one of two vowels, according to position.

(a) When the sound occurs short in a closed syllable, the tendency is to use the nearest English short vowel, i.e. æ as in *lack* læk, which is too close. (See (a) in

Diagram 20.) Thus one hears pæt for pat *patte*, fæs for fas *face*, ʃæs for ʃas *chasse*, kɔɲæk for kɔɲak *cognac*.

(*b*) When the sound occurs long or in a final position, the tendency is to substitute the nearest English vowel occurring under similar conditions, i.e. the ɑ of *calm* kɑːm, *car* kɑː. (See (*b*) in Diagram 20.) Thus one hears l ɑː(r) for l aːr *l'art*, lɑ pɑː(r) for la paːr *la part*, lə mærjaːʒ for lə marjaːʒ *le mariage*, sɑːʒ for saːʒ *sage*, lə sɔldɑː for lə sɔlda *le soldat*.

North-country learners do not, as a rule, have any difficulty with a, for many of them use an a-sound, which is practically the same as French a, in the following circumstances :—

(i) Where the southern English speaker uses æ. Thus they say man *man*, sand *sand*, lam *lamb*, plan *plan*, ant *ant*, while the southern English speaker says mæn, sænd, læm, plæn, ænt.

(ii) In many words where the southern English speaker uses ɑ. Thus they pronounce *past, laugh, dance, plant, aunt*, etc., as past, laf, dans, plant, ant, and not pɑst, lɑf, dɑns, plɑnt, ɑnt, which are the normal pronunciations of the south.

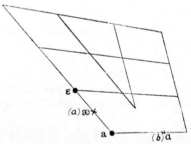

DIAGRAM 20—French a and the English vowels æ and ɑ, which are often substituted for it by English learners.

The difficulty, then, for the southern English learner is to produce a sound intermediate between his æ and his ɑ.

132. Teaching Hints

1. Insist on the correct mouth opening and lip position.

2. *Tongue Position*

(*a*) The learner should try to make his æ a little ɑ-like, with the corners of his lips drawn apart and the tongue held rather loosely. (A " lazy " tongue may result in the necessary lowering.) His attempts should be criticized by the teacher who should suggest the necessary modification : " a little more like ɑ " or " a little more like æ " as the case requires.

(*b*) Often it is possible to use the first element of the diphthong of *I*, but not if the learner says æɪ or ɑɪ. A normal pronunciation of *I* is aɪ, the tongue position of the first element being practically the same as for French a. This first element should be isolated and pronounced with the corners of the lips drawn apart.

(*c*) Some southern English speakers, Cockneys, for example, use a vowel very similar to French a in words like *up, love.*

133. Exercises

(*a*) faː, fa ; vaː, va ; maː, ma ; naː, na ; laː, la ; saː, sa ; faːf, faf ; vaːv, vav ; maːm, mam ; naːn, nan ; saːs, sas ; faːv, fav ; faːm, fam ; faːn, fan ; faːs, fas ; vaːf, vaf ; vaːm, vam ; vaːn, van ; vaːs, vas ; maːf, maf ; maːv, mav ; maːn, man ; maːs, mas ; naːf, naf ; naːv, nav ; naːm, nam ; naːs, nas ; laːf, laf ; laːv, lav ; laːm, lam ; laːn, lan ; laːs, las ; laːʒ, laʒ.

(*b*) la pɛ *la paix*, la fɛːt *la fête*, la bɛːt *la bête*, le kanif *les canifs*, sa e la *ça et là*, la pɛn *la peine*, la lɛn *la laine*, la tɛːt *la tête*, le dwa *les doigts*, fatige *fatigué*, la plas *la place*, la pat *la patte*, la vi *la vie*, la smɛn *la semaine*, l ane *l'année*, la ʃɛːz *la chaise*, lə tapi *le tapis*, lə taba *le tabac*, samdi *samedi*, lə kafe *le café*, la vwasi *la voici*, le bagaːʒ *les bagages*, s ɛ sa *c'est ça*, fɛt sa *faites ça*, sa j ɛ

ça y est, madam *madame*, s ɛt ase *c'est assez*, a midi *à midi*,
ʒamɛ *jamais*, il ɛ la *il est là*, ʒ e swaf *j'ai soif*, deʒa *déjà*,
il ɛ malad *il est malade*, ʒə mɛ sa isi *je mets ça ici*, sa m
fɛ d la pɛn *ça me fait de la peine*, vwala *voilà*, kə fɛ
madam? *Que fait madame?* madam mɛ sa isi *madame met
ça ici*, de fam *des femmes*, ase d plas *assez de place*, dez
ima:ʒ *des images*.

CHAPTER VII

THE FRENCH BACK VOWELS

ɑ (No. 5)

134. *Words containing* ɑ : *âme* ɑːm, *grâce* grɑːs, *Jacques* ʒɑːk, *Jeanne* ʒɑːn, *diable* djɑːbl, *sable* sɑːbl, *fable* fɑːbl, *cas* kɑ, *bas* bɑ, *trois* trwɑ.

135. Description of ɑ

1. The back of the tongue is raised, the front being slightly depressed. In the most usual variety of ɑ the point of highest raising is not as far back as possible, i.e. not so retracted as for Cardinal ɑ. (See Diagram 21.)

2. The raising is very slight : ɑ is therefore an *open* vowel.

3. The mouth is wide open, the corners of the lips drawn more together than for a, but *not* protruded.

136. Comparison with nearest English Sounds

The sound ɑ is not at all difficult for English learners to make. The nearest English vowel is that of *half* hɑf, *palm* pɑm, *alms* ɑmz, which in most cases does quite well, without any modification, for French ɑ. If the learner's English vowel in the above words is too near French a, all he has to do is to modify it in the direction of his ɒ in *on*, *offer*, *otter* (see Diagram 21), without giving any trace of lip-rounding.

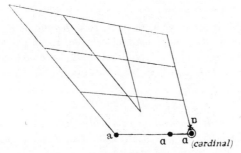

DIAGRAM 21—French ɑ.

137. The difficulty is not in *making* ɑ, but in knowing where to use it, a difficulty which is shared by many French people themselves. Traditional spelling is not helpful, as the following examples show : *table* tabl, *fable* fɑːbl ; *chasser* ʃase, *passer* pɑse ; *donnâmes* dɔnam, *pâle* pɑːl ; *bras* brɑ, *pas* pɑ ; *je bois* ʒə bwa, *le mois* lə mwɑ.

138. In many parts of France (e.g. in the south, in Brittany), in Belgium, in French-speaking Switzerland, ɑ is seldom heard, a vowel intermediate between ɑ and a doing duty for both. This intermediate vowel, (which may be represented by the symbol a), is used by many French speakers where others would use ɑ, e.g. in the terminations *-ation*, *-assion*. Many use it long (where others use the a described in § 130) in final syllables closed by a voiced plosive, e.g. agreaːbl *agréable*, kɔ̃vnaːbl *convenable*, malaːd *malade*.[1]

139. For the distribution of ɑ and a the learner should consult a good pronouncing dictionary and follow it. He will find many French people who distribute the sounds much in the same way as the dictionary indicates, and others who distribute them differently and claim to be right !

[1] See § 417.

140. Exercises

la fɑːbl *la fable*, ʒɑːk *Jacques*, ʒɑːn *Jeanne*, la bɑ *là-bas*,
n ɛ s pɑ? *n'est-ce pas?* madam ɛ la bɑ, n ɛ s pɑ? *madame
est là-bas, n'est-ce pas?* pɑ d taba *pas de tabac*, pɑse par
isi *passez par ici*, ʒə n se pɑ *je ne sais pas*.

ɔ (No. 6)

141. *Words containing* ɔ : *encore* ãkɔːr, *or* ɔːr, *tort* tɔːr,
d'abord d abɔːr, *porte* pɔrt, *Paul* pɔl, *homme* ɔm, *école*
ekɔl, *dot* dɔt, *monotone* mɔnɔtɔn.

142. Description of ɔ.   (See Diagram 22)

1. Normal French ɔ is not a true back vowel.   It has
a distinct central (ə) quality in it, due to the fact that
the tongue raising is in advance of the true back position.
This constitutes the main difficulty of ɔ to English
learners.

2. The tongue is raised to about one-third of the
distance from the lowest to the highest vowel positions.
ɔ is therefore *half-open*.

3. The lips are protruded and rounded and the jaws
well apart.   The lip position may be described as open-
rounded.

143. Comparison with nearest English Sounds

The tendency of English learners is to substitute for
ɔ one of two sounds according to position :—

(*a*) When the sound is followed by r the tendency is
to use English ɔ as in *awe* ɔː, *bore* bɔː (or bɔə), *sort*
sɔːt.   Thus one hears ãkɔː or ãkɔə instead of ãkɔːr
encore, tɔː or tɔə for tɔːr *tort*, sɔːt for sɔrt *sorte*.   This
English ɔ is represented by the same symbol as French

ɔ, but is by no means identical. English ɔ is, in the speech of the majority, a true back vowel (see (*a*) in Diagram 22), and therefore has none of the central quality heard in French ɔ. Another difference is that it requires a closer lip position than French ɔ.

(*b*) When the sound occurs short, the English tendency is to substitute for it the vowel of English *hot* hɒt, *got* gɒt. Thus one hears nɒt for nɔt *note*. ekɒl for ekɔl *école*, pɒm for pɔm *pomme*. English ɒ is a very open back vowel, similar in tongue position to Cardinal ɑ, and produced with little or no lip-rounding. (See (*b*) in Diagram 22.)

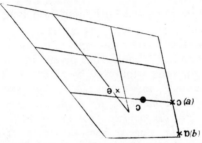

DIAGRAM 22—French ɔ and vowels substituted for it by English learners.

French ɔ differs, then, from the English vowels with which it is confused, in its central quality and its open lip-rounding.

144 Teaching Hints

1. Insist on the correct lip-rounding. An exaggeration of this does no harm.

2. *Tongue Position*

(*a*) The learner who fails to imitate French ɔ can start from either English ɔ or English ɒ, using *open lip-rounding* and introducing a little ə-quality into the sound. Try to do this yourself in the following steps : (i) Pronounce English ɒ as in *on*. (ii) Add open lip-rounding. (iii) Make the sound a little ə-like.

(b) Another method is to start with English ə which is too central. This should be pronounced with open lip-rounding and then modified in the direction of English ɒ or ɔ.

(c) Often it is possible to start from the ʌ of *nut* nʌt, *utter* ʌtə. A common variety of ʌ has a tongue position practically identical with that of French ɔ. All that is needed is to give it the open lip rounding required for French ɔ. This method is not so reliable as methods (a) and (b), as the vowel of *nut* varies a good deal from speaker to speaker.

145. Exercises

ɔ should be practised both short and long :—

(a) ɔf, ɔm, ɔn, ɔs, ɔt, ɔd, ɔʃ, ɔʒ, ɔv, etc.

(b) When the learner can make the sound r satis-factorily, practice should be given in pronouncing syllables containing ɔ followed by r : fɔ:—r, fɔ:r ; mɔ:—r, mɔ:r ; nɔ:—r, nɔ:r ; sɔ:—r, sɔ:r ; mɔrt, fɔrt, sɔrt, pɔrt, etc.

(c) la pɔʃ *la poche*, le pɔʃ *les poches*, la pɔm *la pomme*, ʒ e di pɔm *j'ai dix pommes*, pɔl ɛt isi *Paul est ici*, pɔl ɛ la *Paul est là*, kɔm si kɔm sa *comme ci comme ça*, mɔvɛ *mauvais*, il ɛ ʒɔli *il est joli*, l etɔf *l'étoffe*, mɔnɔtɔn *monotone*, bɔnɔm *bonhomme*, dez ɔm *des hommes*, la bɔn *la bonne*, yn kɔlɔn *une colonne*, yn ɔrlɔ:ʒ *une horloge*, la nɔt *la note*, la pɔst *la poste*.

o (No. 7)

146. *Words containing* o : *côte*, ko:t, *grosse* gro:s, *chose* ʃo:z, *beau* bo, *dos* do, *gros* gro, *mot* mo, *canot* kano, *taureau* tɔro.

147. **Description of o.** (See Diagram 23)

1. The back of the tongue is raised. The modern tendency in French seems to be to use an o which has a tongue position slightly advanced. It is quite unnecessary for English people to imitate this tendency ; and it should be ignored altogether in class teaching.

2. The tongue is raised to about two-thirds of the distance between the lowest and the highest vowel positions. o is therefore a *half-close* vowel.

3. The lips are protruded and rounded leaving an opening large enough to insert the tip of the little finger.

4. Muscular effort of the tongue and lips is necessary.

148. Comparison with nearest English Sounds

A sound similar to French o is heard in Scottish English and in some types of Northern English. The majority of English speakers find it difficult to make a pure o, and substitute for it the diphthong they use in *go* gou, *stone* stoun. This English diphthong varies a good deal from speaker to speaker. In nearly all the varieties heard in educated speech the first element is not a true back vowel at all. It has in it some of the quality of the ɜ of *early* ɜlɪ. (See Diagram 16.)

(*a*) Some speakers actually start with a central vowel of the ɜ type (generally rounded a little), the tongue-raising then moving upwards and backwards towards the u of *move*, but not actually reaching it. (See (*a*) in Diagram 23.) This diphthong could be written phonetically ɜu. It is often described as extreme or affected.

(*b*) Others pronounce the first element of the diphthong with the tongue in a position intermediate between that of ɜ and that of French o ; from this a glide is made towards u. (See (*b*) in Diagram 23.) This diphthong is probably the most common variety heard in normal English. It is represented by the symbols ou, the first symbol standing for an advanced o.

(*c*) Many Cockneys say ʌu or əu. (See (*c*) in Diagram 23.)

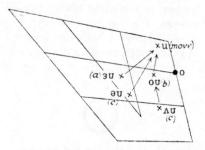

DIAGRAM 23—French **o** and vowels substituted for it by English learners.

Knowledge of the tongue positions of these English vowels explains the difficulty of French **o** to English learners. It also shows that because of the central quality and gliding nature of these sounds they are useless as starting points for teaching French **o**.

149. Teaching Hints

1. If the learner has a back u in words like *move* muv, *pool* pul, start from this. Get him to make it with very strong lip rounding, and then, without moving his lips (use mirror), to make the sound a little ɔ-like, i.e. a little like the vowel of *ought*, *saw*. After a few trials the back of the tongue should drop to the half-close position necessary for French **o**.

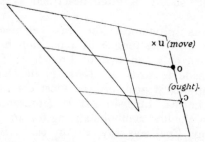

DIAGRAM 24—French **o**, English u, and English ɔ.

2. Another method is to start from English ɔ as in *ought*. Pronounce this with the lips bunched up and thrust forward. Then modify the sound in the direction of u. The back of the tongue should rise from the ɔ position in its attempt to approach u, and an intermediate position should be the result.

3. If the learner does not possess a back u—and many English speakers besides Cockneys do not—a back u should be taught before o. Methods of teaching u are given in § 154. The suggestions for teaching o just given under 1 and 2 above should then be followed.

150. Exercises

o should be practised before a mirror first very long, then short, without any movement of the tongue or lips ; then in syllables with easy consonants. In practising such groups it is important that the lips should be rounded *before* the preceding consonant is pronounced and kept rounded until the end of the syllable :—

(*a*) fo:, fo ; vo:, vo ; mo:, mo ; no:, no ; lo:, lo ; so:, so ; fo:f, fof ; vo:v, vov ; mo:m, mom ; no:n, non ; so:s, sos ; fo:v, fov ; fo:m, fom ; fo:n, fon ; fo:s, fos ; vo:f, vof ; vo:m, vom ; vo:n, von ; vo:s, vos ; mo:f, mof ; mo:v, mov ; mo:n, mon ; mo:s, mos ; no:f, nof ; no:v, nov, etc. fofo, momo, vovo, etc. Much practice is often necessary before the sound is fixed.

(*b*) lə bato *le bateau*, le bo tablo *les beaux tableaux*, l o *l'eau*, sove *sauver*, sote *sauter*, la bote *la beauté*, lez wazo *les oiseaux*, la fo:t *la faute*, a go:ʃ *à gauche*, lez animo *les animaux*, osito *aussitôt*, il fɛ bo *il fait beau*, il fɛ ʃo *il fait chaud*, le ʃapo *les chapeaux*, kɔm il fo *comme il faut*, a kote *à côté*, ʒ e ʃo *j'ai chaud*, də l o ʃo:d *de l'eau chaude*, kə s ɛ dro:l! *Que c'est drôle !* sə n ɛ pɑ d ma fo:t *ce n'est pas de ma faute.*

u (No. 8)

151. *Words containing* u : *toujours* tuʒu:r, *amour* amu:r, *court* ku:r, *autour* otu:r, *rouge* ru:ʒ, *douze* du:z,

doute dut, *soupe* sup, *bouche* buʃ, *douce* dus, *bourse* burs, *lourde* lurd, *bout* bu, *loup* lu, *fou* fu, *doux* du, *coup* ku.

152. Description of u. (See Diagram 25)

1. The back of the tongue is raised. With most French speakers the u is slightly advanced from the true back position.

2. The tongue is raised to the highest back vowel position. u is therefore a *close* vowel.

3. The lips are protruded and strongly rounded, leaving a very small opening between them.

4. Muscular effort on the part of the tongue and the lips is necessary.

153. Comparison with nearest English Sounds

English learners substitute for French u the sound they use in *move, do*. This vowel is generally different from French u in tongue position, in lip position, and in the amount of muscular effort with which it is produced.

1. *Tongue Position*

(*a*) Some English speakers say muv, du with a pure vowel which has a lower tongue position than French u. (See (*a*) in Diagram 25.)

(*b*) Others say muuv, duu, the tongue starting approximately in the position of English ʊ in *put* pʊt, and moving in the direction of English u. (See (*b*) in Diagram 25.)

(*c*) Others start with a more advanced vowel position. Some Cockney speakers, for example, have a close or half-close central vowel as their starting point (unrounded), followed by a short, slightly rounded glide backwards and upwards. (See (*c*) in Diagram 25.)

2. *Lip Position* — English u, ʊu have not the same lip rounding as French u. Normally the protrusion is slight, and the corners of the lips are not drawn closely together.

(*d*) In words like *pour* puːr, *lourd* luːr, *lourde* luɾd, the tendency is to substitute the diphthong ʊə of *poor* pʊə. (See (*d*) in Diagram 25.)

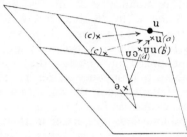

DIAGRAM 25—French u and vowels substituted for it by English learners.

The English learner tends, then, to make a sound for which the tongue position is too low and too advanced, and which requires, in the majority of cases, a movement of the tongue and lower jaw after the sound has been started.

154. Teaching Hints

1. *Lip Position*—Alternate French u and English u or ʊu, drawing attention to the difference in lip position and requiring exaggerated lip rounding for the French sound.

2. *Tongue Position*—To counteract the English tendency to use too advanced a tongue position, aim at a very retracted u and ignore the fact that many French speakers use a slightly advanced variety.

(*a*) Those who use a pure u in English should be required to round the lips very strongly and use more muscular energy. This should result in a slightly higher tongue position.

(*b*) To correct all the other mispronunciations described above, the following plan is recommended. Get the learner to pronounce a word beginning with w followed by his closest *back* vowel, e.g. *walk* wɔk. w is like a short u and has a very retracted tongue position when it occurs before a back vowel like English ɔ. Ask the learner to round his lips very strongly and pronounce *walk* in two syllables. He will lengthen the w to do this, and a good back u should be the result : u — ɔk. This should be said many times before the u is isolated ; and even when the u is pronounced in isolation the learner should think he is about to pronounce ɔ after it. There should be a feeling of tenseness in the muscles of the lips and tongue. The writer has found the above method very successful and knows of no quicker method.

155. Exercises

The learner should practise u in isolation, first long and then short, without any movement from start to finish. (Use mirror.) Then in syllables with easy consonants, rounding the lips strongly during the pronunciation of the entire syllable :—

(*a*) fuː, fu ; vuː, vu ; muː, mu ; nuː, nu ; luː, lu ; fuːf, fuf ; vuːv, vuv ; muːm, mum ; nuːn, nun ; fuːm, fum ; fuːn, fun ; fuːv, fuv ; muːf, muf ; muːn, mun ; muːv, muv ; nuːf, nuf ; nuːm, num ; nuːv, nuv ; etc.

(*b*) After the sound r has been learned : muː—r, muːr ; nuː—r, nuːr ; luː—r, luːr, etc.

(*c*) boku *beaucoup*, la sup *la soupe*, la buʃ *la bouche*, kə fɛt vu? *Que faites vous?* ki ɛt vu? *Qui êtes-vous?* s i vu plɛ *s'il vous plaît*, u ɛt vu? *Où êtes-vous?* lə su *le sou*, su la ʃɛːz *sous la chaise*, tut la smɛn *toute la semaine*, tu sa *tout ça*, ʒ ekut *j'écoute*, ʃe nu *chez nous*, tut a ku *tout à coup*, kɛl bo ʒuːr ! *Quel beau jour !* vəne gute avɛk nu *Venez goûter avec nous*, tuʒuːr *toujours*.

CHAPTER VIII

THE FRENCH FRONT ROUNDED VOWELS AND THE NEUTRAL VOWEL

156. We have noticed that unrounded lips are necessary for the front vowels i, e, ε, a, and rounded lips for the back vowels ɔ, o, u. Now we have to study a series of vowels which resemble front vowels in tongue position and back vowels in lip position.

y (No. 9)

157. *Words containing* y : *mur* my:r, *dur* dy:r, *sûr* sy:r, *bu* by, *lu* ly, *attendu* atɑ̃dy, *une* yn, *lune* lyn, *jupe* ʒyp.

158. Description of y

1. The front of the tongue is raised, but the raising is retracted from the true front position.

2. The tongue is raised to a position a little above half-close.

3. The lips are rounded as for u.

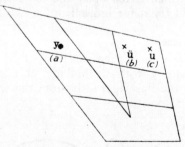

DIAGRAM 26—(*a*) French y, (*b*) English advanced u, (*c*) English normal u.

159. There is no vowel of the y type in normal educated English. The nearest approach to it is the

advanced u (represented by the symbol ü) that many speakers use after the sound j, which has a fronting influence, e.g. bjütɪ *beauty*, əmjüz *amuse*. This advanced u is never so forward as French y. (See Diagram 26.)

160. Teaching Hints

1. Although French y has not the close, front tongue position of French i, the instruction " Round your lips and try your hardest to say i " leads to success in the case of the majority of learners. With the rounding of the lips the tongue takes up a lower position, with the point of highest raising farther back ; and it is only those who make a very special effort to maintain the high position necessary for i who fail to produce a good French y.

2. y can often be taught by starting from the English word *you* ju. Pronounce the *whole* syllable with strong lip rounding. The first sound, when thus rounded and lengthened, is y.

3. English ɪ has often the same tongue position as French y. (See Diagram 19.) ɪ, pronounced with strong lip rounding, should give a good y. In actual practice this method is not very successful, as it often results in a sound which is too open and too retracted. The reader should try it for himself.

161. Exercises

(*a*) Practise y long, then short.

(*b*) Alternate y with i, thinking of i *all the time*, and moving the lips vigorously from the spread to the close rounded position :—

i   y   i   y

This exercise and the two following ones should be practised softly on a monotone, with no break between the sounds.

(*c*) Alternate **y** with **u**, keeping the lips well rounded throughout the exercise :—

(*d*)

The above exercises give excellent tongue and lip practice, so necessary for English pupils, and also practice in passing easily from one vowel position to another without inserting the glottal plosive.

(*e*) Practice in syllables with easy consonants is necessary. Pupils who can make a good isolated **y** often fail to pronounce it correctly in connected speech because they produce the preceding consonant without lip rounding. It is very important that the entire syllable containing **y** should be pronounced with lip rounding. If the preceding consonant is unrounded there is every possibility of an unrounded glide, i.e. **j**, intruding before **y**. *This must be avoided.*

(*f*) fy:, fy; vy:, vy; my:, my; ny:, ny; ly:, ly; sy:, sy; fy:f, fyf; vy:v, vyv; my:m, mym; ny:n, nyn; sy:s, sys; fy:v, fyv; fy:m, fym; fy:n, fyn; fy:s, fys; vy:f, vyf; vy:m, vym; vy:n, vyn; vy:s, vys; my:f, myf; my:v, myv; my:n, myn; my:s, mys; ny:f, nyf; ny:v, nyv; ny:m, nym; ny:s, nys; ly:f, lyf; ly:v, lyv; ly:m, lym; ly:n, lyn; ly:s, lys.

(*g*) Words in which **y** is followed by r should first be practised in two parts : my:—r, sy:—r, dy:—r, py:—r, the parts being brought together when both sounds are satisfactory. The whole syllable should be rounded.

(*h*) Similarly, words in which **y** is preceded by r should first be practised in two parts, care being taken to pronounce r (and any consonant preceding r) with rounded lips : r—y, r—ybā, kr—y, etc.

(*i*) yn dam *une dame*, yn fam *une femme*, yn kle *une clef*, yn plym *une plume*, yn paːʒ *une page*, yn plas *une place*, truve yn plas *trouver une place*, la ʒystis *la justice*, la lyn *la lune*, s ɛ ʒyst *c'est juste*, yn minyt *une minute*, fyme yn pip *fumer une pipe*, pɑ dy tu *pas du tout*, ply du *plus doux*, la ry *la rue*, boku ply dyːr *beaucoup plus dur*, sa m amyːz *ça m'amuse*, suz yn ʃɛːz *sous une chaise*, syr la tabl *sur la table*, dy papje e de plym *du papier et des plumes*, ave vu de plym? *avez-vous des plumes?*, la repyblik *la république*, la vwatyːr *la voiture*, yn tɑːs də te *une tasse de thé*, ply vit *plus vite*, lə byro d post *le bureau de poste*, de legym *des légumes*, dy kote dy luːvr *du côté du Louvre*, ry d rivɔli *Rue de Rivoli*.

ø (No. 10)

162. *Words containing* ø : *précieuse* presjøːz, *eux* ø, *yeux* jø. *mieux* mjø, *deux* dø, *ceux* sø, *peu* pø, *monsieur* məsjø.

163. Description of ø

1. The front of the tongue is raised, but the raising is retracted from the true front position.

2. The tongue is raised to a position about half-way between half-close and half-open.

3. The lips are rounded as for o.

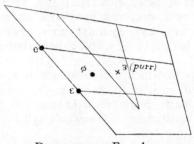

DIAGRAM 27—French ø.

164. There is no vowel of the ø type in normal educated English speech. English people tend to

confuse ø with the ɜ of *purr* pɜ which is a central vowel with no lip rounding. (See Diagram 27.)

165. Teaching Hints

1. Although French ø has not the half-close, front tongue position of French e, the instruction " Round your lips and try hard to say e " helps most learners to make a good ø.

2. Those who produce too close a vowel with the above method should be asked to drop the lower jaw a little, or to try to say ɛ instead of e while the lips are rounded.

3. It is not a good plan to try to teach ø from English ɜ. ɜ, pronounced with lip rounding, results in a sound which is much too retracted.

166. Exercises

(*a*) Practise ø long, then short.

(*b*) Alternate with e, thinking of e *all the time* and moving the lips vigorously from the spread to the rounded position :—

This exercise and the three following ones should be practised softly on a monotone, with no break between the sounds.

(*c*) Alternate with o, keeping the lips rounded to the same degree throughout the exercise :—

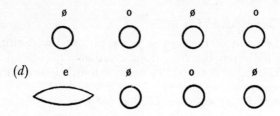

(*e*) Alternate with y :—

y   ø   y   ø

(*f*) Practice in syllables with easy consonants is necessary. The entire syllable containing ø should be pronounced with lip rounding : fø:, fø ; vø:, vø ; mø:, mø ; nø:, nø ; lø:, lø ; sø:, sø ; fø:f, føf ; vø:v, vøv ; mø:m, møm ; nø:n, nøn ; sø:s, søs ; fø:v, føv ; fø:m, føm ; fø:n, føn ; fø:s, føs ; vø:f, vøf ; vø:m, vøm ; vø:n, vøn ; vø:s, vøs ; mø:f, møf ; mø:v, møv ; mø:n, møn ; mø:s, møs ; nø:f, nøf ; nø:s, nøs ; lø:f, løf ; lø:v, løv ; lø:m, løm ; lø:n, løn ; lø:s, løs.

(*g*) dez ø *des œufs*, døz a dø *deux à deux*, døz animo *deux animaux*, pø a pø *peu à peu*, døz ø a la kɔk *deux œufs à la coque*, dø fwa *deux fois*, a pø prɛ *à peu près*, ømɛːm *eux-mêmes*, fot də mjø *faute de mieux*, la kø *la queue*, fɛr la kø *faire la queue*, il va boku mjø *il va beaucoup mieux*, il plø *il pleut*, lə ʒødi *le jeudi*, məsjø, *monsieur*, də bo ʃvø *de beaux cheveux*, il vo mjø *il vaut mieux*, tu le dø ʒuːr *tous les deux jours*, s ɛ pur vu, məsjø *c'est pour vous, monsieur*, k ɛ s kə sa vø diːr? *Qu'est-ce que ça veut dire?* o bo miljø *au beau milieu*, sa s pø *ça se peut*.

œ (No. 11)

167. *Words containing* œ : *sœur* sœːr, *leur* lœːr, *peur* pœːr, *l'heure* l œːr, *beurre* bœːr, *cœur* kœːr, *seul* sœl, *œuf* œf, *bœuf* bœf, *dix-neuf* diznœf, *neuf heures* nœv œːr, *dix-neuf cents* diz nœ sɑ̃.

168. Description of œ

1. The front of the tongue is raised, but the raising is retracted from the true front position.

2. The tongue is raised to a position a little lower than half-open.

3. The lips are open rounded as for ɔ.

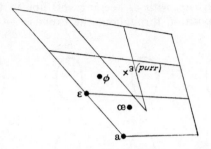

DIAGRAM 28—French œ

169. There is no vowel of the œ type in normal educated English. œ, like ø, is confused by many English learners with the English vowel ɜ of *purr*. (See Diagram 28.)

170. Teaching Hints

The majority of learners will produce a good œ if they round their lips as for ɔ and try to pronounce ɛ. It is important to insist on open lip rounding.

171. Exercises

(*a*) Practise œ long, then short.

(*b*) Alternate with ɛ, thinking of ɛ all the time, and moving the lips vigorously from the unrounded position necessary for ɛ to the open rounded position :—

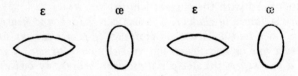

This exercise and the four following ones should be practised softly on a monotone, with no break between the sounds.

(*c*) Alternate with ɔ, keeping the lips in the open-rounded position throughout the exercise :—

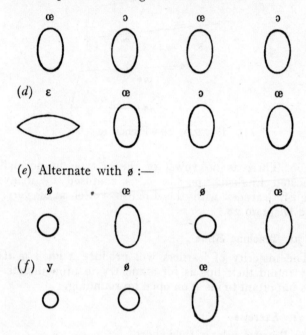

(*g*) Syllables in which œ is followed by r are very numerous and should be frequently practised, first in two parts : œ:—r, sœ:—r, bœ:—r, pœ:—r, kœ:—r. The two parts should then be connected and the syllable pronounced with the correct length.

(*h*) la ʃalœːr *la chaleur*, a la bɔn œːr *à la bonɴe heure*, tut a l œːr *tout à l'heure*, lə profɛsœːr *le professeur*, yn də me sœːr *une de mes sœurs*, pur vu sœl *pour vous seul*, a yn œːr *à une heure*, il ɛ døz œːr *il est deux heures*, dy bœf *du bœuf*, il ɛt œrø *il est heureux*, nu sɔmz œrøːz *nous sommes heureuses*, ave vu dy bœːr? *Avez-vous du beurre?* a nœv œːr *à neuf heures*, ʒ e dø ʃapo nœf *j'ai deux chapeaux neufs*, dit mwa kɛl œːr il ɛ *Dites-moi quelle heure il est*,

il ɛ siz œr dis *il est six heures dix*, dø bœːr *deux beurres*,
yn dəmi œːr *une demi-heure*, diznœf *dix-neuf*, il dəmœːr a
kote *il demeure à côté*, vwala l faktœːr *voilà le facteur*.

The Neutral Vowel ə (No. 12)

172. *Words containing* ə : *je* ʒə, *me* mə, *te* tə, *ce* sə,
fenêtre fənɛːtʳ, *retour* rətuːr, *demander* dəmãde, *premier*
prəmje, *peser* pəze, *justement* ʒystəmã.

173. Description of ə

1. The central part of the tongue is raised.
2. It is raised to a little less than half the distance
between the lowest and highest vowel positions. Notice
in Diagram 29 the position of ə in regard to ø and œ.

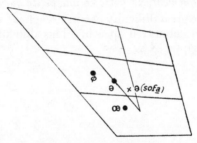

DIAGRAM 29—French ə.

3. The lip position is intermediate between that of
and that of œ. Failure to use lip rounding is a common
fault of English learners. (English ə is produced without
lip rounding.)

174. The above is the description of a fairly average
ə in French. It varies from speaker to speaker. The ə
of some is very ø-like ; of others very œ-like. Others
have an ə which is a little retracted from the position
shown in Diagram 29. This variety is like English ə
except in lip position. (See Diagram 29 for English ə).

175. **Teaching Hints.** French ə is not difficult to
make.

1. The simplest method of teaching it, and quite a successful one, is to ask the learner to pronounce the English neutral vowel as in *sofa* soʊfə, and add lip rounding to it.

2. It is also possible to start from ø and modify it in the direction of œ, or from œ and modify it in the direction of ø.

176. Exercises

(*a*) pə, bə, tə, də, kə, gə, mə, nə, lə, fə, və, sə, zə, ʃə, ʒə.

(*b*) dəmɑ̃de *demander*, lə frɑ̃sɛ *le français*, sə garsɔ̃ *ce garçon*, lə ɥit *le huit*, kə dit vu? *Que dites-vous?* ʒə n kɔ̃prɑ̃ pɑ *Je ne comprends pas*, lə prəmje *le premier*, sɛ̃pləmɑ̃ *simplement*, yn pətit kø *une petite queue*.

177. The great difficulty of ə in French is to know how to use it in connected speech. This difficulty is dealt with in Chapter XX.

CHAPTER IX

THE FRENCH NASALIZED VOWELS

178. Study the following diagrams :—

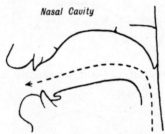

DIAGRAM 30—Oral vowel ɑ.

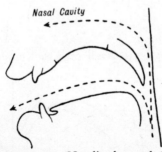

DIAGRAM 31—Nasalized vowel ɑ̃.

For the oral vowel ɑ the soft palate is raised, thus closing the nasal cavity to the air stream which passes through the *mouth only*.

179. For the nasalized vowel ɑ̃ the tongue position is the same as for ɑ. The difference is caused by the

position of the soft palate. For ã it is lowered, and the nasal cavity opened to the air stream, which thus has *two exits*, one through the nose and the other through the mouth.

180. Study the following diagrams of the nasal consonants m, n, and ŋ :—

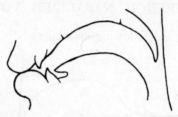

DIAGRAM 32—Nasal consonant **m**.

DIAGRAM 33—Nasal consonant n (dental).

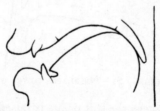

DIAGRAM 34—Nasal consonant ŋ.

Each of them shows a lowering of the soft palate and a *complete closure* in the mouth which makes it impossible for the air to find an exit except through the nose. Here you have the difference between a nasalized vowel and a nasal consonant.

181. The nasalized vowels are not difficult to teach to young beginners. It is advisable to begin with ã since it has practically the tongue position of the corresponding oral vowel which pupils can make without difficulty. They can therefore concentrate on the nasal quality required.

ã (No. 14)

182. *Words containing* ã : *chambre* ʃãːbr, *tante* tãːt, *rentre* rãːtr̥, *ensemble* ãsãːbl, *champ* ʃã, *Jean* ʒã, *cent* sã, *temps* tã, *différent* diferã.

183. Description of ã

1. The position of the tongue and lips for a normal ã is the same as for ɑ. Some speakers have a slightly more retracted tongue position. The modern tendency seems to be towards using a *closer* back vowel position, i.e. to use a nasalized vowel of about the same tongue (not lip) position as English ɔ. Until this practice becomes more widespread among educated speakers foreign learners should use ã.

2. The soft palate is lowered.

184. Teaching Hints

1. The majority of beginners can imitate ã after listening carefully to it. The teacher should make a long ã and ask the pupils what they hear. They will probably say " an ɑ pronounced through the nose ". They should be told that when they make ã the vowel ɑ should be heard *all the time*. Insisting on this prevents them, as a rule, from raising the back of the tongue and adding the velar nasal consonant ŋ, i.e. from saying ãŋ. It must be realized that the nasal quality is not something added after the vowel is finished, but *accompanies* the vowel throughout its length. ã is

really ɑ along with a nasal accompaniment caused by some of the air passing through the nose.

If pupils cannot make ã it is not because they cannot lower the soft palate. They do that every time they pronounce m, n, ŋ. The difficulty is not in lowering the soft palate, but in producing a *vowel* while the soft palate is lowered, i.e. in producing a sound with the air *passing through* nose and mouth cavities *at the same time*.

2. To help those who either cannot give any nasality at all, or who add it after the vowel in the form of a nasal consonant (generally ŋ when the vowel occurs in a final syllable), a good plan is to start with n, which requires a lowering of the soft palate and which pupils can make without any effort.

(*a*) Let them say n rather vigorously and feel the vibration at the sides of the nostrils. Is the same nasal vibration felt in pronouncing l, z, etc.?

(*b*) Then ask them to pass immediately to ɑ, trying to make the nasal vibration continue while producing the vowel, i.e. trying to introduce some of the *n*-quality into the vowel. The result will be ɑ with nasality, i.e. ã. This is a very good method for adults who have difficulty in pronouncing nasalized vowels.

There is a well-known test which reveals at once the presence of a nasal consonant. Close the nostrils between finger and thumb. Try to pronounce ã. If you are really making a nasalized vowel all the time the sound will continue, because the mouth passage is open. If you are saying ãŋ the sound will stop, since the articulation of ŋ closes the mouth passage and your finger and thumb are closing the nasal passage.

(*c*) ã should then be attempted without the help of n.

3. An exercise for the control of the soft palate might now be practised, consisting of the alternation of ɑ and ã with *no change* in the position of the tongue or in the degree of mouth opening or in pitch. Such an exercise helps to make one conscious of the movement

of the soft palate. It should be practised softly, and without a break :

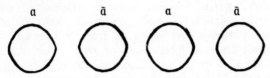

185. **Practice in words**

(*a*) *Nasalized Vowel Final*—The vowel should be made first very long, so that the effect of any movement of the tongue can be better heard ; then short :

bã:, bã ; sã:, sã ; tã:, tã ; lã:, lã ; dã:, dã ; gã:, gã.

(*b*) *Nasalized Vowel Non-final*—There is here a tendency to insert a nasal consonant after the nasalized vowel, even when the learner has not seen the conventional spelling. For *semble* he is tempted to say sã:mbl instead of sã:bl. The lips are brought together for b while the soft palate is still lowered for ã:. This produces m. For the same reason m is also often inserted before p, e.g. lã:mp is said instead of lã:p. For *santé* the English learner wants to say sãnte instead of sãte ; for *demander* dəmãnde instead of dəmãde, the tongue preparing to articulate t or d while the soft palate is still lowered for the nasalized vowel. Hence the insertion of n which has the same place of articulation as t or d. Similarly, after a nasalized vowel occurring before k or g the sound ŋ is often inserted, *inquiet* being pronounced ɛ̃ŋkjɛ instead of ɛ̃kjɛ, *langue* lã:ŋg instead of lã:g. The only way to banish this kind of mistake is to require the learner to make a pause after the nasalized vowel pronounced unduly long ; then to eliminate the pause when he can avoid the nasal consonant ; and finally to pronounce the word with the correct length :

sã:—bl, sã:bl ; sã:—te, sã:te, sãte ; dəmã:—de, dəmã:de, dəmãde ; ã:—tã:—dy, ã:tã:dy, ãtãdy.

(c) lə tã *le temps*, il fɛ bo tã *il fait beau temps*, tu l tã
tout le temps, trã:t *trente*, karã:t *quarante*, swasã:t
soixante, ʒãvje *janvier*, sɛptã:br *septembre*, nɔvã:br
novembre, desã:br *décembre*, vãdrədi *vendredi*, dimã:ʃ
dimanche, tã mjø *tant mieux*, lə frãsɛ *le français*, l ãglɛ
l'anglais, dit sa ã frãsɛ *Dites ça en français*, dit sa ãn
ãglɛ *Dites ça en anglais*, kɔmã sa va? *Comment ça va?*
ʒə m ã vɛ *je m'en vais*, vu vuz ãn ale *vous vous en allez*,
ã vule vu? *En voulez-vous?* s ɛ si frã *c'est six francs*, s ɛt
ãtãdy *c'est entendu*, la sal d atã:t *la salle d'attente*, a la
kãpaɲ *à la campagne*, ʒyst a tã *juste à temps*, sa depã *ça
dépend*, s ɛ dy tã pɛrdy *c'est du temps perdu*, nə vu derãʒe
pa *Ne vous dérangez pas*, kɔmã vuz aple vu? *Comment vous
appelez vous?* il fɛ boku d vã *il fait beaucoup de vent*,
k ã pãse vu? *Qu'en pensez-vous?* apsɔlymã vrɛ *absolument
vrai*, ʒ e suvã fɛ sa *j'ai souvent fait ça*, ãn ãglətɛ:r *en
Angleterre*, ã frã:s *en France*, ãn atãdã *en attendant*, defã:s
d ãtre *défense d'entrer*, le ʃãz elize *les Champs-Elysées*.

õ (No. 15)

186. *Words containing* õ : *nombre* nõ:br, *Londres* lõ:dr,
bon bõ, *long* lõ, *pardon* pardõ.

187. Description of õ

1. The back of the tongue is raised.

2. It is raised to a position about midway between
the lowest and highest vowel positions. It will be seen
from the diagram that õ is not the nasalized form of

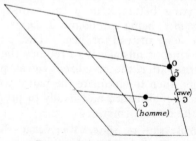

DIAGRAM 35—French õ.

French ɔ as in *homme*, but of a vowel intermediate between English ɔ as in *awe* and French o. It is nearer to French o than to French ɔ. Some phoneticians use ō to represent it, and the International Phonetic Association would have done the same if it were not for the fact that when denasalization occurs with liaison the nasalized vowel is replaced by ɔ as in *bonne* : bõ *bon*, bɔn ãfã *bon enfant*.

3. The lip position is intermediate between that of ɔ and that of o, but nearer to that of o.

4. The soft palate is lowered.

188. **Teaching Hints**

If pupils fail to imitate õ

1. Start from o and let them try to make it with nasal vibration (prefixing n if necessary).

2. As an exercise for the control of the soft palate let them alternate o õ o õ keeping the same lip position throughout.

3. Let them also alternate õ with ã :

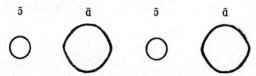

189. **Practice in Words**—It is important that the lips should be rounded whilst pronouncing the consonant preceding õ.

(*a*) *Nasalized Vowel Final*—The vowel should be pronounced first very long, with no movement after the sound is begun, then short : dõ:, dõ; sõ:, sõ; fõ:, fõ; lõ:, lõ; mõ:, mõ; bõ:, bõ; nõ:, nõ.

(*b*) *Nasalized Vowel Non-final*—The following words should be practised first in two parts with a pause between each syllable ; and then normally, when the tendency to insert a nasal consonant has disappeared : tõ:—be, tõ:be, tõbe ; mõ:—te, mõ:te, mõte ; mõ:—d, mõ:d ; lõ:—g, lõ:g.

(c) atãsjõ *attention*, lə põ d aviɲõ *le pont d'Avignon*, mõte le baga:ʒ *monter les bagages*, tu l mõ:d *tout le monde*, lə garsõ *le garçon*, la kɛstjõ *la question*, pãse dõ:k ! *Pensez donc* !, vu vu trõpe *vous vous trompez*, swasãt e õz frã *soixante et onze francs*, ʒyst o fõ *juste au fond*, lez ãvirõ *les environs*, ʒə vu dmãd pardõ *je vous demande pardon*, də tu mõ kœ:r *de tout mon cœur*, ʒə dmœr a lõ:dr *je demeure à Londres*, uvre la, dõ:k *Ouvrez-la, donc*, ʒə sɥi kõtã d vu *je suis content de vous*, tu l mõd desã *tout le monde descend*, bõʒu:r ! *Bonjour* !, də la kõfity:r *de la confiture*.

ɛ̃ (No. 13)

190. *Words containing* ɛ̃ : *simple* sɛ̃:pl̥, *dinde* dɛ̃:d, *coin* kwɛ̃, *main* mɛ̃, *faim* fɛ̃, *bien* bjɛ̃, *fin* fɛ̃.

191. Description of ɛ̃

1. The front of the tongue is raised.

2. It is raised to a position about midway between that for a and that for ɛ. ɛ̃ is not the nasalized form of ɛ, but rather of a vowel similar to that used by Southern English speakers in *man* mæn. (See Diagram 36.)

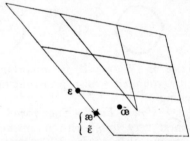

DIAGRAM 36—French ɛ̃ and œ̃.

3. The lip position is the same as for ɛ.
4. The soft palate is lowered.

192. Teaching Hints

If learners fail to imitate ɛ̃

1. Start from æ and let them try to produce it with nasality (prefixing n if necessary).

2. As an exercise for the control of the soft palate let them alternate æ and ɛ̃, keeping the same lip and tongue position throughout.

3. Practice in alternating ɛ̃ with ɑ̃ and ɔ̃, already known, will help them to make the necessary differences :

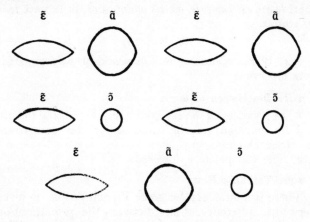

ɛ̃   ɑ̃   ɛ̃   ɑ̃

ɛ̃   ɔ̃   ɛ̃   ɔ̃

ɛ̃   ɑ̃   ɔ̃

These exercises should be practised *gently* and on a monotone, with no break between one vowel and the next.

193. Practice in Words

(*a*) *Nasalized Vowel Final*—The vowel should be pronounced very long, then short : bɛ̃:, bɛ̃ ; fɛ̃:, fɛ̃ ; pɛ̃:, pɛ̃ ; sɛ̃:, sɛ̃ ; tɛ̃:, tɛ̃ ; vɛ̃:, vɛ̃ ; mɛ̃:, mɛ̃ ; nɛ̃:, nɛ̃.

(*b*) *Nasalized Vowel Non-final*—sɛ̃:—pḷ, sɛ̃:pḷ (no m !) ; sɛ̃:—t, sɛ̃:t (no n !) ; l ɛ̃—stɑ̃, l ɛ̃stɑ̃ (no n !) ; ɛ̃:—kjɛ, ɛ̃:kjɛ, ɛ̃kjɛ (no ŋ !).

(*c*) lə kwɛ̃ *le coin*, la mɛ̃ *la main*, vɛt ɑ̃ *vingt ans*, vwasi vɛ̃ frɑ̃ *voici vingt francs*, lə prɛ̃tɑ̃ *le printemps*, sɛ̃ plym *cinq plumes*, ʒ e grɑ̃ fɛ̃ *j'ai grand'faim*, dɑ̃ l trɛ̃ *dans le train*, s ɛ bjɛ̃ di *c'est bien dit*, vɛ̃tsɛ̃ sɑ̃tim *vingt-cinq centimes*, sɛ̃kɑ̃t su *cinquante sous*, swasɑ̃t kɛ̃:z *soixante-quinze*, kɛ̃z frɑ̃ vɛ̃tsɛ̃:k *quinze francs vingt-cinq*, katrə vɛ̃ ɔːz *quatre-vingt-onze*, a bjɛ̃to *à bientôt*, sɛ̃ minyt a atɑ̃ːdr *cinq minutes à attendre*, a l ɛ̃stɑ̃ *à l'instant*, tjɛ̃! *Tiens!*, ɛ̃finimɑ̃ *infiniment*, ʒə vø bjɛ̃ *je veux bien*, ɑ̃fɛ̃ *enfin*, trɛ bjɛ̃ *très bien*, də mwɛz ɑ̃ mwɛ̃ *de moins en moins*, dɑ̃ l ʒardɛ̃ *dans le jardin*, lə trɛ̃ d pari *le train de Paris*, il ɛ bjɛ̃ kɔ̃tɑ̃ *il est bien content*, bjɛ̃n ɑ̃tɑ̃dy *bien entendu*, lə vɛ̃ ɛ kɔ̃pri *le vin est compris*, mɛ̃tnɑ̃ *maintenant*, tu le matɛ̃ *tous les matins*.

œ̃ (No. 16)

194. *Words containing* œ̃ : *humble* œ̃ːbl, *parfum* parfœ̃' *brun* brœ̃, *un* œ̃.

195. Description of œ̃

1. In a variety of œ̃ very commonly heard, the tongue and lip position are the same as for the oral vowel œ. (See Diagram 36.)
2. The soft palate is lowered.

196. Teaching Hints

There is a tendency for some French people to make very little difference, if any, between the pronunciation of *brun* and *brin* : it is brɛ̃ for both words. This tendency should be noticed by English learners, but not imitated. œ̃ and ɛ̃ should be kept distinct. If pupils fail to imitate œ̃—

1. Start from œ trying to introduce nasality into it. (Prefixing n if necessary.)
2. Alternate œ and œ̃, keeping the same open-rounded lip position and the same tongue position throughout.
3. Alternate œ̃ with the other three nasalized vowels. This gives helpful practice in passing easily from one vowel to another and in making the necessary difference :

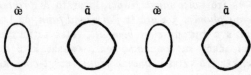

œ̃　　　ɑ̃　　　œ̃　　　ɑ̃

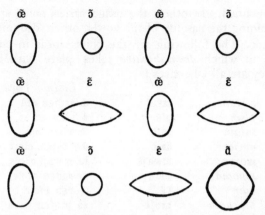

197. Practice in Words—It is important that the lips should be rounded for the consonant preceding œ̃.

(*a*) *Nasalized Vowel Final*—okœ̃ *aucun*, kɔmœ̃ *commun*, parfœ̃ *parfum*, brœ̃ *brun*, ʃakœ̃ *chacun*, kɛlkœ̃ *quelqu'un*.

(*b*) *Nasalized Vowel Non-final*—œ̃:bl *humble*, lœ̃di *lundi*.

(*c*) s ɛt œ̃ ʃapo *c'est un chapeau*, ɑ̃ vwasi œ̃ ʒɔli *en voici un joli*, œ̃ frɑ̃ sɛ̃ sɑ̃tim *un franc cinq centimes*, vɛ̃t e œ̃ su *vingt et un sous*, tu d œ̃ ku *tout d'un coup*, œ̃n œf a la kɔk *un œuf à la coque*, lə parfœ̃ *le parfum*, œ̃ grɑ̃ magazɛ̃ *un grand magasin*, œ̃ ku d œ:j *un coup d'œil*, œ̃n ɔtɔbys *un autobus*.

Pronunciation of the liaison forms of words ending in the letter *n*

198. When words ending with the letter n occur finally in a group, or before a word beginning with a consonant sound, the n has no sound-value : it is merely a sign that the preceding vowel is nasalized : *plein* plɛ̃, *bien* bjɛ̃, *un* œ̃, *bon* bɔ̃, *certain* sɛrtɛ̃, *aucun* okœ̃.

199. In many words of this kind the vowel loses its nasality when liaison occurs (i.e. when a sound-value is given to the n before a vowel). In others, nasality is retained. In others the usage varies, some speakers retaining the nasality of the vowel, others dropping it.

200. The following are the chief words in common use in which *denasalization* takes place with liaison. They are all adjectives :

		Liaison Form
certain	sɛrtɛ̃	œ̃ sɛrtɛn ãfã
plein	plɛ̃	ã plɛn ɛːr
vilain	vilɛ̃	œ̃ vilɛn ɔm
ancien	ãsjɛ̃	œ̃n ãsjɛn elɛːv
moyen	mwajɛ̃	lə mwajɛn aːʒ
soudain	sudɛ̃	œ̃ sudɛn efɔːr
vain	vɛ̃	œ̃ vɛn efɔːr
prochain	prɔʃɛ̃	sõ prɔʃɛn uvraːʒ
bon	bõ	œ̃ bɔn argymã ; bɔn ãfã

All front consonants (margin note)

Notice that the liaison form of these adjectives is pronounced in exactly the same way as the feminine form.

201. The following are the chief words in common use in which the nasality of the vowel is kept when liaison occurs. They have no feminine which could serve as the liaison form :—

en	ã	ãn atãdã ; nu n ãn avõ ply
bien	bjɛ̃	bjɛ̃n ase ; bjɛ̃n ãtãdy
rien	rjɛ̃	rjɛ̃n a fɛːr

202. In the following words usage varies. The first liaison form given (in which the nasality of the vowel is kept) is the more common and is therefore recommended to English learners :

		Liaison Forms	
mon	mõ	a mõn avi	a mɔn avi
ton	tõ	tõn õːkl̩	tɔn õːkl̩
son	sõ	sõn ɛ̃teliʒãːs	sɔn ɛ̃teliʒãːs
on	õ	õn atã	ɔn atã
un	œ̃	œ̃n ɔm	œn ɔm
aucun	okœ̃	okœ̃n ɛ̃terɛ	okœn ɛ̃terɛ

203. *Quelqu'un* and *chacun* are seldom linked with the following word, and not at all in conversation : *chacun à son gout* ʃakœ̃ a sɔ̃ gu, *quelqu'un est arrivé* kɛlkœ̃ ɛt arive.

204. It is important to notice that if it is possible to make a pause [1] after the word ending in *n*, i.e. if the following word is not very closely linked in meaning with it, liaison does not occur : *Je n'ai rien ou presque rien* ʒə n e rjɛ̃ | u prɛskə rjɛ̃. *Donnez-en aux enfants* dɔnez ɑ̃ | oz ɑ̃fɑ̃. *Il est bien* (comfortable) *ici* il ɛ bjɛ̃ | isi. *Il est bien* (indeed) *ici* il ɛ bjɛ̃n isi.

---

[1] The pause need not actually be made.

CHAPTER X

THE FRENCH VOWELS
IN UNSTRESSED SYLLABLES

205. The reader has no doubt realized, while listening to French speakers, that French has many more than the sixteen vowel sounds which are absolutely essential. Our present study of the vowels has been confined to the values they have when they occur in stressed positions.

206. The general tendency in languages is for stressed vowels to keep their " strong " quality, and for absolutely unstressed ones to be replaced by shorter and weaker ones ; sometimes to disappear altogether.

207. In some languages, for example in English, where there is rather a big difference between the amount of energy expended on different syllables, this tendency to vowel weakening is very strongly developed, especially in the conversational style of speech. When stress is absent, most English vowels are prone to desert their positions and make tracks towards ə, losing length and strength on the way. Some, having reached the position of ə, disappear entirely :

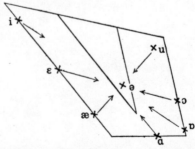

DIAGRAM 37—Vowel weakening in English.

A few examples will make this clear : *and* ænd is pronounced ənd, ən and n in unstressed syllables, e.g. *You and I* 'ju ənd 'aɪ, *merry and bright* 'mɛrɪ ən 'braɪt, *bread and cheese* 'brɛd n 't∫iz.

has hæz is pronounced həz, əz, z, s in unstressed syllables, e.g. *The money has gone* may be pronounced ðə 'mʌnɪ həz 'gɒn, ðə 'mʌnɪ əz 'gɒn, ðə 'mʌnɪ z 'gɒn. *It has gone* may be pronounced ɪt həz 'gɒn, ɪt əz 'gɒn, ɪt s 'gɒn.

at æt is ət in *at home* ət 'hoʊm.

saint seɪnt is sənt, snt or sn in *St. Paul's Churchyard* : s(ə)n(t) 'pɔlz t∫ɜt∫'jɑd.

was wɒz is wəz or wz in *I was there* aɪ w(ə)z 'ðɛə.

from frɒm is frəm or frm in *a present from Yarmouth* ə 'prɛznt fr(ə)m 'jɑməθ.

for fɔ is fə in *That's for you* 'ðæt s fə 'ju.

208. Many English people do not realize the great use they make of ə in unstressed positions : they imagine that *and* is invariably pronounced ænd, *from* invariably frɒm, etc. Some deliberately try to avoid too frequent a use of ə. They condemn it as a modern development, the result of modern carelessness, and determine that it must be resisted if the spoken language is to be saved from degradation. And yet this vowel-weakening is perfectly natural in a language like English, and has been going on for many generations. It is well to bear it in mind, for it is the cause of one of the Englishman's great difficulties in his acquisition of foreign languages. It is responsible for such mis-pronunciations as parəgraf for paragraf, kəmāse for kɔmāse, ʒenərəl for ʒeneral, səpɔrte for syporte, mɔnətɔn for mɔnotɔn, ədrɛs for adrɛs, ərive for arive.

209. A Frenchman learning English finds the use of ə in unstressed positions extremely difficult. He prefers to say 'æz 'gʊd 'æz 'goʊld instead of əz 'gʊd əz 'goʊld *as good as gold* ; 'aɪ 'wɒz 'æt 'hoʊm 'frɒm 'tu 'tu 'θri instead of aɪ wəz ət 'hoʊm frəm 'tu tu (or tə) 'θri *I was at home from two to three* ; 'seɪnt 'pɔlz 'kæ'θi'dræl

instead of snt ˈpɔlz kəˈθidrl *St. Paul's Cathedral.* Why? Because in French the great difference between strong and weak syllables, characteristic of English, does not exist. A distinct beat could be given to each syllable of the following French words, and each syllable is pronounced with a strong vowel : *national* ˈnaˈsjoˈnal, *cathédrale* ˈkaˈteˈdral, *enchanteur* ˈɑ̃ˈʃɑ̃ˈtœːr, *commencement* ˈkɔˈmɑ̃sˈmɑ̃. Their English equivalents require one strong beat and two short, weak taps : *national* ˈnæʃnl, *cathedral* kəˈθidrl, *enchanter* ɪnˈtʃɑntə, *commencement* kəˈmɛnsmənt. Notice the strong vowel in the stressed syllable of the English words, and the frequency of ə or the complete absence of a vowel in the weak syllables.

210. Stress is much more evenly distributed, then, among the syllables of a French word than among those of an English one, with the result that French vowels have more stability than English ones. But they are not absolutely stable. They do undergo changes in unstressed positions, but of a much less radical kind than those occurring in English. Is it necessary to study these changes?

211. In the case of the great majority of French vowels the modifications they undergo in unstressed syllables are slight, and it is quite unnecessary for the foreigner to make them.

212. Take i, for example. Many Frenchmen use a more open i in an unstressed than in a stressed position. The i which occurs in the non-final, i.e. unstressed, syllables of the following words or groups of words is generally more open than the i which occurs finally : iˈsi *ici*, fiˈni, *fini*, il ɛ parˈti *il est parti*, midi e dˈmi *midi et demi*. In teaching English learners, however, it is better to insist always on a very close i, at any rate in the early stages. If pupils depart from it slightly, later on, well and good. But it is not good policy to invite them to depart from it. Their natural tendency in unstressed positions is to forsake the close i position

for the lowered and retracted one of English ɪ, a tendency which should receive no encouragement.

213. Other French vowels also are changed slightly by the absence of stress and by the nature of surrounding sounds ; but with the exception of e and ɛ it is perhaps unnecessary to examine these changes.

214. *Unstressed* e—In unstressed positions the e described in § 120 sounds un-French. If you listen to a Frenchman pronouncing the following words unemphatically you will notice that non-final, unstressed e is distinctly more open than final, stressed e : *gaieté*, geᶦte, *bébé* beᶦbe, *pénétrer* peneᶦtre, *élever* elᶦve, *libérer* libeᶦre, *piéton* pjeᶦtõ, *vérité* veriᶦte, *téléfoner* telefoᶦne.

215. Unstressed e is often called e moyen. It is written phonetically with the same symbol as stressed e.

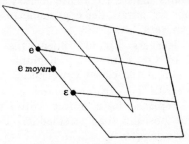

DIAGRAM 38—e moyen.

216. Certain words are nearly always pronounced in connected speech with e moyen. They are words like *mes*, *tes*, *ses*, *les*, *des*, *ces*, which occur almost invariably in non-final unstressed positions : *les enfants* lez ɑ̃ᶦfɑ̃, *des Français* de frɑ̃ᶦsɛ, *mes affaires* mez aᶦfɛːr. (When *les* occurs finally, as in *Sauvez-les* ! sove ᶦle ! the tendency is to use close e and not e moyen.)

217. It is necessary to notice that there exists another pronunciation for *mes*, *tes*, *ses*, etc., besides that with e moyen. Some speakers use ɛ, which is often heard in acting, singing, public speaking, teaching, and even

in conversation. According to some authorities this pronunciation, at any rate in conversation, is artificial and not to be imitated. Discussing the pronunciation of these monosyllabic words Martinon writes [1] : " A la vérité, beaucoup d'acteurs, de professeurs, d'orateurs, s'efforcent encore d'articuler *lès hommes* lɛz ɔm, et essayent de résister à l'usage universel, mais cette prononciation est absolument conventionelle. Elle est bonne tout au plus dans le chant, qui a des exigences propres : quand on parle, on ne saurait prononcer *mes* dans *mes sœurs* autrement que dans *mesdames*, où il est certainement fermé.[2] Même après un impératif, le pronom *les*, devenu tonique, est aussi fermé que l'article dans l'usage universel. Sans doute les poètes continuent à faire rimer *donne-les* avec *poulets* ou *balais* mais c'est affaire à eux, et on ne voit pas pourquoi *les* aurait deux prononciations, une en prose, une en vers."

218. As learners become fluent they should be encouraged to use e moyen. Beginners should be required to aim at the closer vowel in all positions.

219. *Unstressed* ɛ — In unstressed syllables ɛ also tends to be replaced by a moyen vowel which has a *higher* tongue position than stressed ɛ. Sometimes it is as close as e moyen.

220. The use of stressed ɛ in all positions sounds stiff and unnatural to a French ear. *pêche* is pronounced pɛːʃ. In *pêcher* the ɛ is closer, but is written with the same symbol : pɛˡʃe. Similarly with *prête* prɛːt and *prêter* prɛˡte, *chaîne* ʃɛːn and *déchaîner* deʃɛˡne, *aime* ɛːm and *aimer* ɛˡme, *traître* trɛːtr̩ and *traîtresse* trɛˡtrɛs, *il l'est* il l ˡɛ and *il est médecin* il ɛ metˡsɛ̃, *elle en avait* ɛl ɑ̃n aˡvɛ and *elle en avait beaucoup* ɛl ɑ̃n avɛ boˡku.

221. Learners who have attained a certain fluency should be encouraged to use ɛ moyen.

---

[1] Martinon : *Comment on Prononce le Français*, p. 54.
[2] Really moyen.

222. With the exception of e and ε, then, it is advisable that all French vowels should be pronounced by the English learner as if they were in stressed positions. Stressed and unstressed vowels have not exactly the same quality in French ; but the slight differences that exist are in most cases negligible. If the English learner *makes an effort* to produce them his English habit of vowel-weakening is apt to carry him much too far.

The French Consonants

223. The following table gives the French consonants, indicating the *place* of articulation (bi-labial, labio-dental, dental, etc.), and the *manner* in which they are articulated (plosive, nasal, etc.).

224. Table of French Consonants

Manner of Articulation	Place of Articulation								
	Bi-Labial	Labio-dental	Dental	Alveolar	Post-Alveolar	Palatal	Velar	Uvular	Glottal
Plosive .	p b		t d				k g		(ʔ)
Nasal .	m		n			ɲ			
Lateral .			l						
Rolled .				r				ʀ	
Fricative .		f v		s z	ʃ ʒ			ʁ	(h)
Semi-vowel	w ɥ					j [ɥ]	[w]		

NOTE.—Symbols occurring in two columns represent sounds with two essential articulations. The secondary articulation is shown in square brackets. Symbols in round brackets represent sounds which are not essential in French. Three **r**-sounds are indicated, but only one is necessary in speaking French.

225. For all consonants except the nasals, the soft palate is raised, the air finding an exit through the mouth only. (This fact will be taken for granted in the descriptions of the consonants which follow.)

CHAPTER XI

PLOSIVE CONSONANTS

226. In forming plosive consonants the mouth passage is completely closed at some point and then opened so that the air pent up behind the closure escapes suddenly.

227. There are six essential plosive consonants in French : p, t, k, which are voiceless ; and their voiced counterparts b, d, g. ʔ occurs in rare circumstances. p, t, and k will be described first, and the special difficulties they present to English learners will be explained.

The French Voiceless Plosive Consonants

p

228. For p the lips completely stop the passage through the mouth ; air is compressed behind the stop and escapes with an explosive sound when the stop is released.

229. As an isolated sound p presents no difficulty. But when it occurs before a vowel in a stressed syllable many English learners find it difficult to pronounce in the French way.

230. A comparison between the normal Southern English way of pronouncing p as in *park*, *pass*, *pole*, *port*, *paw*, etc., and the normal French way of pronouncing p as in *Pâques*, *pas*, *paix*, *pomme*, etc., may help the learner.

English p of *park*.

231. The first upright line in the diagram below (No. 39) represents the bringing together of the lips for p, and the second the separation, which is

immediately followed by the plosion. During the stop (i.e. that part of the consonant formed while the lips are together) no voice is heard. (A straight horizontal line represents this absence of voice.) After the lips are separated no voice is heard for a short time, but air is being emitted ; i.e. the sound of *h* is being pronounced. (A straight horizontal line represents this **h**.) Then the vowel ɑ begins (represented by a horizontal wavy line denoting voice) :

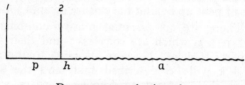

DIAGRAM 39—Aspirated **p**.

232. When the sound **h** is inserted between the plosion of a consonant and the following vowel the consonant is said to be aspirated. **p**, **t**, and **k** are generally aspirated in English before vowels in stressed syllables.

233. Voiceless plosives are aspirated in many other languages, e.g. in Danish, Swedish, some kinds of German.

234. The above diagram (No. 39) shows a normal amount of aspiration in English. Some Southern English speakers use more ; many Northern speakers use less or none at all.

235. Pronounce fairly energetically a number of words like *peak*, *pain*, *pear*, *park*, *pork* ; *tar*, *take*, *tear*, *talk*, *two* ; *car*, *care*, *cork*, *cool*. Can you hear any aspiration?

French **p** of *Pâques*

236. The lips are brought together with more energy than for English **p**. The stop is voiceless, as in English.

After the smart separation of the lips no sound of *h* is heard : the vowel starts immediately after the plosion [1] :

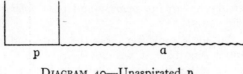

DIAGRAM 40—Unaspirated p.

French t and k are also unaspirated.

237. Voiceless plosives are unaspirated in many other languages, e.g. Italian, Spanish, Russian, South German.

238. Is the English learner making a serious mistake when he aspirates p, t, and k in speaking French? Not by any means so serious as it would be if he were speaking one of the numerous languages which exist in which the omission or insertion of h is significant. In many Indian, Chinese, and African languages pairs of words exist which are distinguished solely by the presence or absence of aspiration. In Bengali, for example, thɑ:l means *plate*, and tɑ:l *palm-fruit*. In Burmese phe: means *father*, pe: *foot-rule* ; khu: means *caterpillar*, ku: *to help*.

239. An Englishman, speaking French, would not be misunderstood if he strongly aspirated every p, t, and k ; but the cumulative effect of all this aspiration would be very un-French and very unpleasant. English learners should try, then, to eliminate the sound of *h* after p, t, and k, and let the vocal cords vibrate for the vowel immediately after the plosion.

240. In the case of young pupils there is no need to give special pronunciation exercises for the elimination of aspiration. After a little ear-training they will readily hear the difference between pʰɑ and pɑ, tʰɑ and tɑ, kʰɑ and kɑ ; and they soon learn to regulate the breath-

---

[1] Some French people aspirate their plosives slightly, but it is not typical to do this.

stream so that no h intervenes between consonant and vowel. London pupils, whose aspiration is often of a very fricative nature, should be required to separate the articulating organs *smartly* and pass *quickly* to the following sound.

241. An adult can often *hear* the aspiration he uses, but cannot eliminate it without help. He should try to make a p rather like his English b in *bark*, at the same time using *more energy* in the bringing together and separation of the lips. This attempt to make a b-like p generally results in a good unaspirated p, since English initial b is quite unaspirated and is pronounced with very little, if any, voice. Diagrammatically it might be represented thus :—

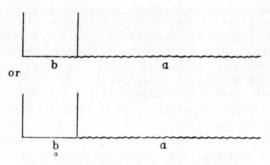

DIAGRAM 41—Initial b in English.

242. **Exercises**

(*a*) pi, pe, pɛ, pa, pɑ, pɔ, po, pu, py, pø, pœ, pə, pɛ̃, pɑ̃, pɔ̃, pœ̃.

(*b*) la paːʒ *la page*, la pɛ *la paix*, lə pɛ̃ *le pain*, lə palɛ *le palais*, lə panje *le panier*, la paːr *la part*, la pɔm *la pomme*, lə pɛːr *le père*, lə pɔ̃ *le pont*, la pɔst *la poste*, puse *pousser*, poze *poser*, pike *piquer*, la pɑ̃se *la pensée*, ʒə n sɛ pɑ *je ne sais pas*, pur pɑse l tɑ̃ *pour passer le temps*, a pɛn *à peine*, la pœːr *la peur*, pø d tɑ̃ *peu de temps*, pɔl paːr pur pari *Paul part pour Paris*.

t

243. t is made in the same manner as p, but the closure is formed by placing the tip of the tongue against the upper teeth, and not against the teeth-ridge, as in English :

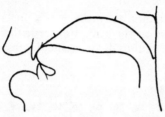

DIAGRAM 42—French t with tip of tongue against upper teeth.

Some French people place the tip against the lower teeth, the articulation taking place between the blade and the teeth-ridge :

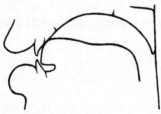

DIAGRAM 43—French t with tip of tongue against lower teeth.

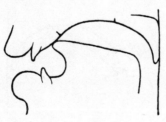

DIAGRAM 44—English t.

This difference in the place of articulation has a distinct effect on the character of the sound. The difficulty is not to make the difference, but to remember to make it. It is a good plan to let English pupils practise the sound at first with the tip of the tongue just *between* the teeth.

244. An attempt to make a t a little like English initial d as in *do*, at the same time articulating with more energy than is required for d, should result in a strong unaspirated t.

245. Exercises

(*a*) ti, te, tɛ, ta, tɑ, tɔ, to, tu, ty, tø, tœ, tə, tɛ̃, tɑ̃, tɔ̃, tœ̃.

(*b*) it, et, ɛt, at, etc.

(*c*) la tabl *la table*, tɑ̃to *tantôt*, lə tapi *le tapis*, tot u taːr *tôt ou tard*, la tɑːs *la tasse*, le tɛ̃ːbr *les timbres*, tire *tirer*, tɔ̃be *tomber*, tu l mɔ̃ːd *tout le monde*, tuʒuːr *toujours*, tut a ku *tout à coup*, tut a fɛ *tout à fait*, tut a l œːr *tout à l'heure*, la sal d atɑ̃ːt *la salle d'attente*, lə prɛ̃tɑ̃ *le printemps*, təne vu drwɑ ! *Tenez-vous droit* !

k

246. k is made in the same manner as p and t, but the closure is formed by raising the back of the tongue to touch the fore part of the soft palate.

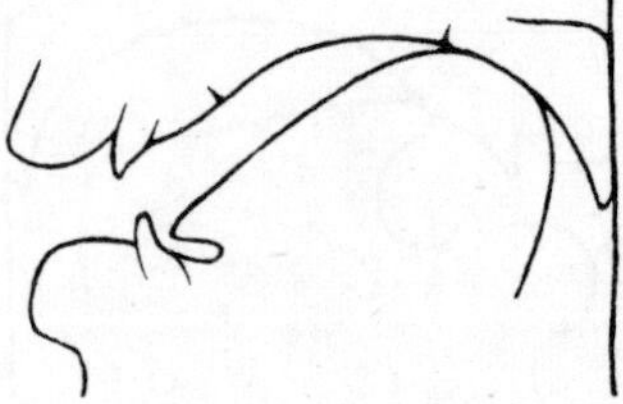

DIAGRAM 45—French k.

247. Before a front vowel, as in ki *qui*, ke *quai*, kɛ̃:z *quinze*, the articulation is more forward than indicated in the above diagram. It is often described as being more forward than in English before front vowels. If this is so, it is of no practical importance.

248. Before a back vowel as in ka *cas*, ãkɔ:r *encore*, ku *coup* the articulation is more retracted than that shown in the above diagram.

249. The use of a series of k sounds (and of g sounds) whose point of articulation depends on the tongue position of the following vowel is common to both English and French, and therefore need not trouble the learner.

250. Some French speakers exaggerate the fronting of k and g *before front vowels* to such an extent that the velar articulation is replaced by a palatal one.[1] This very pronounced fronting need not be imitated by English learners.

251. An attempt to make a k a little like English initial g as in *go*, at the same time articulating with more energy, should result in a strong unaspirated k.

252. Exercises

(a) ki, ke, kɛ, ka, kɑ, kɔ, ko, ku, ky, kø, kœ, kə, kɛ̃, kɑ̃, kɔ̃, kœ̃.

(b) yn ka:ʒ *une cage*, yn kart *une carte*, yn kart pɔstal *une carte postale*, œ̃ ku *un coup*, tut a ku *tout à coup*, l ekɔl *l'école*, ã tu kɑ *en tout cas*, kɔm il fo *comme il faut*, də tu kote *de tous côtés*, dez ø a la kɔk *des œufs à la coque*, a la kãpaɲ *à l la campagne*, dəpɥi kã? *Depuis quand?* kɛlkə kɛstjɔ̃ *quelques questions*, fɛr la kø *faire la queue*, ki ɛ la? *Qui est là?*

---

[1] The symbol for the voiceless palatal plosive is c ; that for the voiced palatal plosive ɟ. These sounds have the same tongue position as ɲ. See Diagram 48.

ʔ

253. The formation of ʔ has been described in Chapter IV. (See §§ 66–70.)

254. English learners who have formed the habit of using ʔ in unemphatic French before words which begin with a vowel should try the following plans for avoiding it :

1. In the phonetic texts you are reading insert a linking mark ‿ [1] between two words, the second of which begins with a vowel, to remind you that there should be no abrupt beginning to the vowel, but a gradual glide on to it from the preceding sound :

ɛl‿a‿ublie sa prɔmɛs (not ɛl ʔa ʔublie sa prɔmɛs) *elle a oublié sa promesse.* il‿ɛt‿ale‿a‿amjɛ̃ (not il ʔɛt ʔale ʔa ʔamjɛ̃) *il est allé à Amiens.* il kɔ̃dɥizɛt‿œ̃n‿ elefɑ̃‿a l abrœvwaːr (not il kɔ̃dɥizɛt ʔœ̃n ʔelefɑ̃ ʔa l abrœvwaːr) *il conduisait un éléphant à l'abreuvoir.* il sɔ̃t‿arive‿a‿aviɲɔ̃‿a‿ɔ̃z‿œːr (not il sɔ̃t ʔarive ʔa ʔaviɲɔ̃ ʔa ʔɔ̃z ʔœːr) *ils sont arrivés à Avignon à onze heures.* il‿ɛ deʒa‿ɑ̃‿o (not il ʔɛ deʒa ʔɑ̃ ʔo) *il est déjà en haut.*

2. If the above plan is not a sufficient check rewrite the troublesome passages in such a way that each syllable following a space begins with a consonant :

ɛ lau blie sa prɔmɛs. i lɛ ta leaa mjɛ̃. il kɔ̃dɥizɛ tœ̃ nelefɑ̃a labrœvwaːr, etc.

3. Practise *gliding* from one vowel position to another :

ei,	eɛ,	ea,	eɑ,	eɔ,	eo,	eu, etc.
ɛi,	ɛe,	ɛa,	ɛɑ,	etc.		
ɛ̃i,	ɛ̃e,	ɛ̃ɛ,	ɛ̃ɑ,	etc.		
ɑ̃i,	ɑ̃e,	ɑ̃ɛ,	ɑ̃a,	etc.		
ɔ̃i,	ɔ̃e,	ɔ̃ɛ,	ɔ̃a,	etc.		
œ̃i,	œ̃e,	œ̃ɛ,	œ̃a,	etc.[2]		

[1] This mark is used in many phonetic texts to indicate liaison.

[2] See also §§ 161, 166, 171 for other exercises for passing gradually from one vowel to another.

You should then have no difficulty in saying : le ɔ̃:z *les onze*, œ ɔlɑ̃dɛ *un Hollandais*, de ibu *des hiboux*, œ̃n ɑ̃fɑ̃ ɔbeisɑ̃ *un enfant obéissant*, lɥi e ɛl *lui et elle*, œ nɔ̃ ɛ̃kɔny *un nom inconnu*, brœ e vɛ:r *brun et vert*, yn mezɔ̃ a vɑ̃:dr *une maison à vendre*, səlɔ̃ ɛl *selon elle*, dəmɑ̃dɔ̃ a œ̃n aʒɑ̃ *demandons à un agent*.

The French Voiced Plosive Consonants

b, d, g

255. b, d, and g have the same place of articulation as p, t, and k. They are difficult for English learners because they are pronounced in a different way from English b, d, and g in the matter of *voice*.

256. The sounds b, d, and g can be pronounced in three different ways in regard to voice : they may be fully voiced, partially voiced, and pronounced with no voice at all :

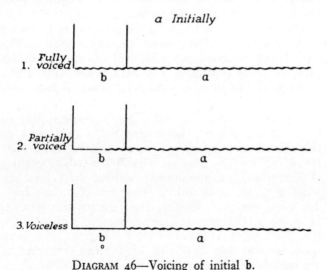

DIAGRAM 46—Voicing of initial b.

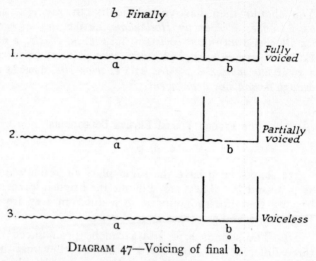

DIAGRAM 47—Voicing of final b.

257. The important difference between b̥ and unaspirated p is that the former is pronounced with much less energy than the latter.

258. In French, b, d, and g are normally fully voiced in all positions. The voicing begins as soon as the articulating organs come into contact, and continues until they are separated, e.g. barb *barbe*, dɛ̃:d *dinde*, gard *garde*, lã:g *langue*, sabo *sabot*, dədã *dedans*, argo *argot*.

259. In English, b, d, and g are fully voiced only in intervocalic positions, the voicing being very weak in the case of some speakers : habə *harbour*, ladə *larder*, igə *eager*. Initially they are partially voiced, as in (*a*) 2 (Diagram 46), or pronounced without voice (i.e. like weak p, t, k), as in (*a*) 3 (Diagram 46) : bɑk *bark*, dɑk *dark*, gou *go*. Finally, they are partially voiced, as in (*b*) 2 (Diagram 47), or pronounced without voice (i.e. like weak p, t, k), as in (*b*) 3 (Diagram 47) : kræb *crab*, læd *lad*, læg *lag*. An Englishman's attempt to say barb *barbe* often results in something like ᵖbarbᵖ.

260. English people find it difficult to voice b, d, and g fully in initial and final positions. In order to speak French well they must learn to do this. They must attempt also to give more *vigorous* voicing to b, d, and g in intervocalic positions.

261. It is especially difficult to practise full voicing while making the stop of b, d, or g, since the stops of these sounds cannot be easily prolonged. Fricatives like z are easier to voice : they have no closure and can therefore be prolonged without special effort ; moreover their voicing is more distinctly heard than that of a plosive. The learner is therefore advised, before attempting fully voiced b, d, and g, to try to make a fully voiced fricative, e.g. z. Methods of learning to do this are given in § 330.

262. Even after following these methods, the learner may find it necessary to attempt the plosives in steps. The following are suggested :

1. Pronounce energetically the neutral vowel ə with hand on throat so that the vibration of the vocal cords is felt.

2. While making ə bring the lips *nearly* together. Try *at the same time* to continue the vowel, and this will help you to continue to produce voice.

3. While pronouncing ə, bring the lips gently into contact. Use extra muscular energy and try to continue the voice while the lips are closed. If you can do this you are making a fully voiced b.

263. **Exercises**

(*a*) bi, be, bɛ, ba, etc.

ib, eb, ɛb, ab, etc.

(*b*) bõ *bon*, bjɛ̃ *bien*, boku *beaucoup*, bõte *bonté*, bebe *bébé*, bɛ̃ *bain*, bɑ *bas*, bato *bateau*, biːz *bise*, la barb *la barbe*, yn bõːb *une bombe*, le ʒɑ̃ːb *les jambes*.

(*c*) Practise fully voiced d in the same way.

(*d*) di, de, dɛ, da, etc.

id, ed, ɛd, ad, etc.

(e) dəmɛ̃ *demain*, dədɑ̃ *dedans*, dəbu *debout*, dəɔːr *dehors*, dəpɥi lɔ̃tɑ̃ *depuis longtemps*, dɔne lə oz ɑ̃fɑ̃ *donnez-le aux enfants*, dɑ̃ la ry *dans la rue*, dit mwa *dites-moi*, defɑ̃s d ɑ̃tre *défense d'entrer*, dɛrjɛr vu *derrière vous*, dəmɑ̃de *demander*, desɑ̃ːbr *décembre*, dezire *désirer*, dəsu *dessous*, dəsy *dessus*, dø u trwa *deux ou trois*, diznœf *dix-neuf*, dɔrme bjɛ̃ *Dormez bien*, yn dɛ̃ːd *une dinde*, yn tablə rɔ̃ːd *une table ronde*, yn fam almɑ̃ːd *une femme allemande*, boku d mɔ̃ːd *beaucoup de monde*, ʒə m dəmɑ̃ːd *je me demande*, pɑ trɔ grɑ̃ːd *pas trop grande*.

(f) Practise fully voiced g in the same way.

(g) gi, ge, gɛ, ga, gɑ, gɔ, go, gu, gy, gø, gœ, gə, gɛ̃, gɑ̃, gɔ̃, gœ̃.

(h) ig, eg, ɛg, ag, ɑg, etc.

(i) grɛ̃pe *grimpez*, gute *goûtez*, grate *grattez*, grɔ̃de *grondez*, galɔpe *galopez*, garde vu bjɛ̃ də tɔ̃be *Gardez-vous bien de tomber*, yn lɑ̃ːg *une langue*, yn bag *une bague*, œ̃ djalɔg *un dialogue*, œ̃ katalɔg *un catalogue*, le vag *le vagues*.

CHAPTER XII

NOTES ON THE FRENCH NASAL CONSONANTS

264. For nasal consonants there is a complete closure in the mouth at some point, the soft palate is in its lowered position and the air-stream passes out through the nasal cavity. (See Diagrams 32, 33, 34.)

265. The French nasal consonants are m, n, and ɲ.

266. m is articulated in exactly the same way as in English. Sometimes the sound is voiceless in French, e.g. in *prisme*, *rhumatisme* prism̥, rymatism̥, though one also hears prism, rymatism, and prizm, rymatizm.

267. n is dental, like t and d. It is alveolar in English.

268. ɲ does not occur in English. The nearest approach to this sound in English is the group nj as in *spaniel* spænjəl.

269. **Description of ɲ**

1. The blade of the tongue is down, the tip touching the lower teeth.
2. The front of the tongue is in contact with the hard palate.
3. The soft palate is lowered.
4. The sound is voiced.

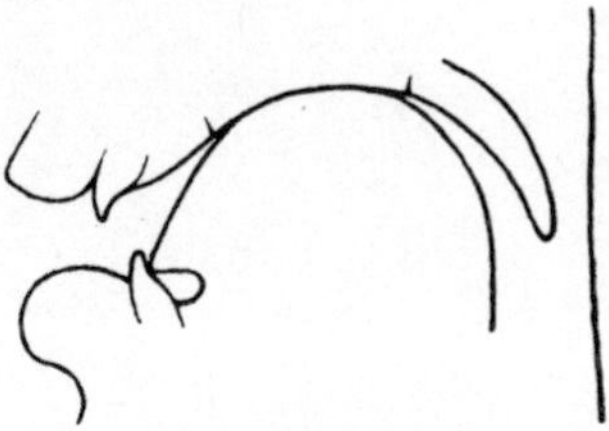

DIAGRAM 48—ɲ.

270. Teaching Hints

An attempt to produce the sound n with the tip
and blade down (held down, if necessary) so that the
articulation cannot be made on the teeth-ridge, but is
forced back on to the hard palate, should result in ɲ.
Some learners manage to produce ɲ by starting from
English ŋ as in *long* lɒŋ (see Diagram 34) and trying to
articulate the sound much further forward. The faint
j glide which is heard on moving the front of the tongue
away from the hard palate is an essential part of ɲ.

271. Exercises

(*a*) iɲ, eɲ, ɛɲ, aɲ, etc.

(*b*) iɲi, eɲe, ɛɲɛ, aɲa, etc.

(*c*) diɲ *digne*, la viɲ *la vigne*, a la kɑ̃paɲ *à la campagne*,
la mɔ̃taɲ *la montagne*, œ̃ pɛɲ *un peigne*, l aɲo *l'agneau*,
lə põ d aviɲõ *le pont d'Avignon*, œ̃n ɛspaɲɔl *un Espagnol*,
la vil də bulɔɲ *la ville de Boulogne*.

CHAPTER XIII

l-SOUNDS

272. The sound l is articulated by raising the tip of the tongue to touch the teeth or teeth-ridge. This contact forms only a partial closure of the air passage, since the air can escape at one or both sides of the tongue. To feel this lateral escape alternate n with a vigorous voiceless *l*, keeping the tip of the tongue in the same place for both sounds. (The escape of air is greater for ḷ than for l and can therefore be better felt.)

273. Many different varieties of *l*-sounds are used in speech. For our purpose it will be helpful to examine those used in English and then to compare the French variety with them.

A. The *l*-sounds used in English

1. Clear *l*

274. Pronounce the word *leap* several times, and then try to isolate the *l*-sound. Pronounce it many times in isolation. You will probably notice—

(*a*) That the tip and blade of the tongue are raised to touch the teeth-ridge.

(*b*) That the sound has a certain vowel quality running through it : approximately that of the ɪ of *is*.

It has this because the front of the tongue is raised as for ɪ while the contact for l is being made. The continuous line in the diagram below (No. 49) shows the position of the l of *leap*, the dotted line that of the ɪ of *is*. In the former case the tip and blade are raised ; in the latter the tip and blade are lowered. The rest of the tongue occupies the same position for both sounds :

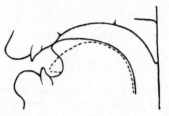

DIAGRAM 49— —— l of *leap*. ······· ɪ of *is*.

This *l*-sound is called *clear* because of the front vowel quality which runs through it.

275. *Usage*—Clear *l* is used by the majority of English people before a vowel : *leave, lift, letter, like, lock, lord, look*. Its clearness is not the same in these words. It is probably clearest in *leave*; a little less clear in *lift, letter, like*; neutral in *lock, lord, look*. For practical purposes, however, these shades of clearness may be neglected, and it may be simply stated that the *l* is clear in all these words.

2. Dark *l*

276. Pronounce the word *people* several times. Isolate the *l*-sound. Pronounce it in isolation many times. You will probably notice—

(*a*) That the tip of the tongue is raised to touch the teeth-ridge as for clear *l*.

(*b*) That the sound has a certain vowel quality running through it : approximately that of the ʊ of *put*. It has this because the back of the tongue is raised as for ʊ while the contact for l is being made. The continuous line in the diagram below (No. 50) shows the position of the l of *people*, the dotted line that of the ʊ of *put*. In the former case the tip and blade are raised ; in the latter they are lowered. The rest of the tongue occupies about the same position for both sounds :

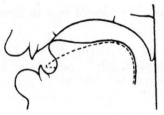

DIAGRAM 50— ——— l of *people*. ······· ʊ of *put*.

This *l*-sound is called *dark* [1] because of the back vowel quality which runs through it.

277. *Usage*—Dark *l* is used by the majority of English people—

(*a*) Finally, e.g. in *simple, people, table, oval, supple, apple, little, pale, pile, pill, peal, pull.*

(*b*) Before consonants, e.g. in *filled, belt, wealth, self, golf, bulb, failed, fold.*

The degree of darkness varies, just as the degree of clearness varies in the case of clear *l*. The darkest variety is probably that which occurs finally and functions as a syllable, e.g. the *l* of *people, simple,* etc. For practical purposes, however, degrees of darkness may be neglected, and the *l* may be simply described as dark in the positions defined above.

3. Exercises

278. (*a*) Alternate clear *l* with dark *l*, keeping the tip of the tongue in the same place : lᴵ, lᵁ, lᴵ, lᵁ. You should feel a distinct movement in the main part of the tongue in passing from clear to dark *l*.

(*b*) Try to pronounce *leave, lift, letter, like, lock,* etc., with a dark *l*. Many Scots and Americans do this.

(*c*) Pronounce *simple, people, table, pale, peal, field, belt,* etc., with a clear *l*. Some Irish and Northern English do this. The natural tendency of Frenchmen, Germans, Swedes, and many others is to pronounce in this way.

[1] Special symbol ɫ.

B. The l-sound used in French

279. Description

1. The tip of the tongue for the *l* of *lit* is placed against the upper teeth,[1] and at the same time the front of the tongue is raised as for the vowel i. This *l* is therefore a little " clearer " than the English *l* of *leap*.

DIAGRAM 51—French l with tip of tongue raised.

2. The air escapes at one or both sides of the closure.
3. The sound is generally voiced.

French *l* is clear in *all* positions. It varies slightly in clearness, e.g. the *l* of *lit* is clearer than the *l* of *loup*. The different shades of clearness need not trouble the English learner, since his own clear *l* varies in exactly the same way.

Teaching Hints and Exercises

280. Before vowels the clear *l*-sound the English learner uses will do quite well in French.

281. Finally and before consonants, i.e. where the English speaker uses a dark *l*, special exercises are generally needed.

282. Practise making a very clear *l* in isolation, i.e. aim at pronouncing the French vowel i, at the same time making the contact for l :

li, li, li, li.

---

[1] The tip may also be placed against the lower teeth, the partial closure of the air-passage being made by the blade in contact with the teeth-ridge.

283. *Clear l Finally, Preceded by a Vowel*—Pronounce clear *l* after all the French vowels, first with a pause after the vowel, then joining the sounds up :

(i) i — l, il; e — l, el; ɛ — l, ɛl; a — l, al; ɑ — l, ɑl; ɔ — l, ɔl; o — l, ol; u — l, ul; y — l, yl; ø — l, øl; œ — l, œl; ɛ̃ — l, ɛ̃l; ã — l, ãl; õ — l, õl; œ̃ — l, œ̃l.

(ii) la vil *la ville*, lə kɔl *le col*, s ɛ fasil *c'est facile*, s ɛ difisil *c'est difficile*, yn fil *une file*, œ̃ kɔlɔnɛl *un colonel*, œ̃ bɔl *un bol*, l ɛl *l'aile*, lə kanal *le canal*, fidɛl *fidèle*, œ̃ ʃval *un cheval*, s ɛt inytil *c'est inutile*, bjɛ̃ mal *bien mal*, l ekɔl *l'école*, natyrɛl *naturel*, nasjɔnal *national*, sivil *civil*, pɛrsɔnɛl *personnel*, sãtral *central*, kɔmynal *communal*, ɛspaɲɔl *espagnol*, l etɛ̃sɛl *l'étincelle*, gradɥɛl *graduel*, ideal *idéal*, mɔbil *mobile*, lə rɔsiɲɔl *le rossignol*, l irõdɛl *l'hirondelle*, spesjal *spécial*, ləkɛl *lequel*, lakɛl *laquelle*, lə ʒurnal *le journal*, œ̃ mɔdɛl *un modèle*, inegal *inégal*, l animal *l'animal*, l epoːl *l'épaule*, madmwazɛl *mademoiselle*, a la bɛl etwal *à la belle étoile*, l ɔtɛl də vil *l'Hôtel de Ville*.

284. *Clear l Finally, Preceded by a Consonant Sound*—

(i) If the preceding consonant is *voiceless* the *l* is generally completely voiceless : l artik̹l *l'article*, œ̃ sɛrk̹l *un cercle*, de buk̹l *des boucles*, la pãtuf̹l *la pantoufle*, sɛ̃ːp̹l *simple*, l egzãːp̹l *l'exemple*, sup̹l *souple*, spɛktak̹l *spectacle*, trip̹l *triple*, sjɛk̹l *siècle*, par egzãːp̹l! *par exemple* !

(ii) If the preceding consonant is a *voiced plosive* the *l* is often partially voiceless. (This need not be marked in a phonetic transcription) : ɛmaːbl *aimable*, avœgl *aveugle*, ãːgl *angle*, ɛːgl *aigle*, la tabl *la table*, la rɛːgl *la règle*, ãsãːbl *ensemble*, kõːbl *comble*, dubl *double*, efrwɑjaːbl *effroyable*, l õːgl *l'ongle*, ɛ̃dispãsaːbl *indispensable*, admiraːbl *admirable*, penibl *pénible*, sãblaːbl *semblable*, l epɛ̃ːgl *l'épingle*, adɔraːbl *adorable*, ɛ̃pɔsibl *impossible*.

285. Here it is convenient to refer to the pronunciation of words like those given in § 284 (*article*, *spectacle*,

impossible, admirable, etc.) when they occur medially in a group. Note the following points :—

(i) When followed immediately by a vowel the *l* is fully voiced : œn admira:bl ɔratœ:r *un admirable orateur,* yn ɛtɛrminabl ɑ̃gwas *une interminable angoisse,* œ spɛktakl inwi *un spectacle inouï,* le pɑ̃tufl etɛ trɔ grɑ̃:d *les pantoufles étaient trop grandes,* l artikl ɛ trɛz ɛterɛsɑ̃ *l'article est très intéressant,* ɛl ɛt ɛmabl e dus *elle est aimable et douce,* il ɛt ɛ̃dispɑ̃sabl a mɔ̃n œ:vr *il est indispensable à mon œuvre,* œn imœbl a mɔ̃ gu *un immeuble à mon goût,* sɛ̃pl e inɔsɑ̃ *simple et innocent,* mɛtrə lə kɔ̃:bl a sɔ̃n œ:vr *mettre le comble à son œuvre,* lə pœpl almɑ̃ *le peuple allemand.*

(ii) When followed immediately by a consonant sound the orthographic *e* which ends such words is given a sound-value : yn admirablə lɛtr̥ *une admirable lettre,* yn ɛtɛrminablə nɥi *une interminable nuit,* œ mirɑ:klə də grɑ:s *un miracle de grâce,* de pɑ̃tuflə də satɛ̃ *des pantoufles de satin,* l artiklə də fɔ̃ *l'article de fond,* œn imœblə nœf *un immeuble neuf,* yn sɛ̃plə flœ:r *une simple fleur,* il nu kɔ̃:blə d elɔ:ʒ *il nous comble d'éloges,* s ɛt ɛ̃pɔsiblə də fɛr sa *c'est impossible de faire ça,* lə ply bo spɛktaklə dy mɔ̃:d *le plus beau spectacle du monde,* lə pœplə də pari *le peuple de Paris,* la rɛglə de partisip *la règle des participes.*

(iii) In familiar conversation words of very common use are pronounced without both ə and l before a word beginning with a consonant sound : ɛ̃pɔsib də fɛr sa *impossible de faire ça,* artik də pari *article de Paris,* de pɑ̃tuf də satɛ̃ *des pantoufles de satin,* i m sɑ̃b kə nɔ̃ *il me semble que non,* œ sɛ̃p sɔlda *un simple soldat,* lə pœp də pari *le peuple de Paris.*

These contracted forms are not so usual as in the case of words which, when pronounced in isolation, end in r preceded by a consonant sound, e.g. *pauvre, maître, mettre, arbre.* (See § 306 (iii).)

286. *Clear l Followed by a Consonant Sound* :

(i) i — lf, ilf ; ɛ — lf, ɛlf ; a — lp, alp ; ɑ — lg, ɑlg ; ɔ — ld, ɔld ; o — lk, olk ; u — lm, ulm ; y — ln, yln, etc.

(ii) sœlmã *seulement*, tu l mõ:d *tout le monde*, il fɛ bo tã *il fait beau temps*, ʒə m apɛl ʒã *je m'appelle Jean*, kõsylte *consulter*, la difikylte *la difficulté*, malgre lɥi *malgré lui*, vu dve l kɔnɛ:tr̩ *vous devez le connaître*, kɛlkəfwa *quelquefois*, kɛlkœ̃ *quelqu'un*, lez almã *les Allemands*, yn bul də nɛ:ʒ *une boule de neige*.

CHAPTER XIV

r-SOUNDS

287. A knowledge of the formation of the *r*-sound used by the majority of English speakers in speaking English should help the reader to understand better the difficulties of the *r*-sound in French.

English Fricative *r* [1]

288. **Description**

1. The tip of the tongue is raised to the back part of the teeth-ridge.
2. The passage is narrowed at that point, but not sufficiently to cause much friction.
3. The sound is voiced.

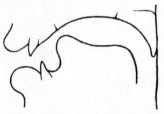

DIAGRAM 52—English fricative *r* (ɹ)

r-sounds used in French

289. In French three *r*-sounds may be heard: 1, r, lingual rolled; 2, ʁ, uvular fricative; 3, ʀ, uvular rolled.

---

[1] Special symbol ɹ.

1. Lingual Rolled *r* (r)

290. Description

1. The tip of the tongue is raised to the teeth-ridge and so held that it vibrates up and down against the teeth-ridge as the air-stream passes through the mouth.

2. r is generally voiced.

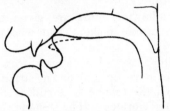

DIAGRAM 53—Lingual rolled r (r).

Usage

291. The lingual rolled *r* is not the *r*-sound commonly heard in Paris and the large towns, though there it may be heard frequently on the stage and on the concert platform. Although it is gradually giving way to the uvular variety it may perhaps still be considered as the *r* in common use in the small towns and villages of France. For this reason it is looked upon as provincial by those who do not use it.

292. r is the sound which English learners are generally recommended to use. Like the English fricative *r* it is articulated by the tip of the tongue. Many English people can already make it, and most of them have heard it used by speakers from Scotland, Ireland, Wales, and Northern England. There are Southern English speakers who use a weakened variety of r between two vowels, as in *thorough* θʌrə, *hurry* hʌrɪ, *foreign* fɒrɪn, *tomorrow* təmɒrou, and before final l and n as in *carol* kærl, *barren* bærn.

293. Teaching Hints

1. Let the class hear a well-made r. The majority will probably be able to imitate it at once.

2. Those who fail to make the sound, naturally become self-conscious and hold their tongues stiffly if asked to attempt it in the presence of the whole class. Much time will be saved if each pupil who cannot at once imitate r is given into the charge of a fellow-pupil who makes it well and who will guarantee to teach it out of class-time.

294. The following hints are given to help those teachers who cannot make r and who prefer it to a uvular variety :

1. In making r, as we have already seen, the tip of the tongue has to move up and down, striking against the teeth-ridge. If the tongue is as stiff as a poker the tip will refuse to vibrate. The tongue must be held *loosely*.

2. Start with English fricative *r*. Try to hold the tongue loosely and let the air come in sudden jerks. If this fails to make the tip vibrate, change the position of the tip slightly, advancing it, retracting it, lowering it slightly, raising it slightly, until it is in a position where it is capable of vibrating. It is useless to keep the tip of the tongue in the same position while trying to make r.

3. Prefix θ to English fricative *r*, still holding the tongue loosely. The tip should be drawn back suddenly after the θ. During this retraction the tip is often felt to vibrate.

4. Pronounce the English word *thorough* θʌrə with strong breath force, withdrawing the tip of the tongue suddenly after θ. You may find it possible to trill the *r* in this intervocalic position.

5. Avoid attempting the sound when you are very tired, and never attempt it for long at a time.

6. When a series of taps can be made diminish the force of breath so that there is no breathiness in the sound, but just a series of distinct little taps.

7. Practise r very long, then with two or three taps

only. It should never be strongly rolled in connected speech, unless for emphasis.

8. For practice in all positions, see § 301 (v)–§ 308, substituting r for ʁ.

2. Uvular Fricative *r* (ʁ [1])

295. Description

1. The back of the tongue is raised towards the uvula, leaving a fairly wide passage, so that very little friction is caused as the air passes through. The front of the tongue is depressed.

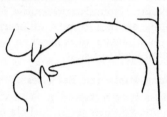

DIAGRAM 54—Uvular fricative *r* (ʁ).

2. You will see from the diagram that the tongue position is not very different from that required for a very retracted open back vowel, i.e. from that of Cardinal ɑ.

3. The sound is generally voiced.

Usage

296. The uvular fricative *r* is nowadays very commonly heard in Paris and other large towns of the north. Many use it in unemphatic speech in all positions. In emphasis it is often replaced by the uvular rolled *r*. (See § 309.) English learners are often advised to look upon ʁ as an unpleasant sound unworthy of their

---

[1] This special symbol is used only in this chapter. Elsewhere the symbol r is used, the reader interpreting it as r or ʁ or R according to his choice of *r*-sound.

attention. This is probably because their efforts to produce it often result in a disagreeable, scrapy noise which a Frenchman refuses to accept as an *r* of any kind. The widespread use of ʁ among educated speakers marks it as very French, and for that reason it commends itself to many English learners.

297. ʁ is dealt with in this book before the uvular rolled *r* because of its spreading use in France and because it provides an excellent starting point for attacking the uvular rolled *r* if learners decide to adopt the latter sound.

298. Teachers of French pronunciation should learn one of the uvular *r*-sounds (preferably ʁ), and should give their pupils an opportunity of hearing it. Some pupils find ʁ (or ʀ) easier to make than ɾ. Such pupils should be encouraged to use it.

299. Teaching Hints and Exercises

1. Start with a very retracted ɑ. You will notice that while making this you can see the whole of the uvula.

2. Keeping the tip of the tongue against the lower teeth, raise the back of the tongue from the ɑ position until the *end* of the uvula is hidden from view (use

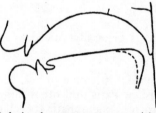

DIAGRAM 55—Relation between tongue positions of a retracted ɑ (shown by dotted line) and ʁ.

mirror), and try to retain some of the quality of ɑ. The sound you make with the tongue in this position should be a *very weak* fricative with a rather vowel-like quality—ʁ. Try to reduce the friction to a minimum. (If you unconsciously introduce one or two taps, as some learners often do, you are making a rolled uvular *r* : ʀ.)

3. Pass from ʁ to ɑ again.

300. Some students find it a help to regard ʁ as of the same type of sound as the English fricative *r* in *red*. For the English sound it is the *tip* of the tongue that is raised to form the narrowing ; for ʁ the tip is depressed and the *back* is raised to form the narrowing. In both sounds the friction is *extremely weak*.

301. ʁ *Between Two Vowels*.

(i) Repeat the slight movement of the back of the tongue (described above), keeping the tip against the lower teeth and maintaining the same mouth-opening : ɑʁɑ, ɑʁɑ, ɑʁɑ.

(ii) Practise in the same way ɔʁɔ, oʁo, uʁu, using throughout the lip-rounding required for the vowel.

(iii) aʁa, ɛʁɛ, eʁe, iʁi.

(iv) yʁy, øʁø, œʁœ (lip-rounding as for the vowel).

(v) Words containing intervocalic ʁ : buʁo *bourreau*, buʁe *bourrer*, tɔʁo *taureau*, byʁo *bureau*, puʁɛ *pourrait*, ɛʁe *error*, ɑ̃ʁyme *enrhumer*, dɑ la ʁy *dans la rue*, la ʁut *la route*, aʁɛte *arrêter*, aʁive *arriver*, eʁɛte *éreinté*, iʁige *irriguer*, atiʁe *attirer*, paʁi *Paris*, l aʁab *l'arabe*, kɔʁiʒe *corriger*, la difeʁɑ̃ːs *la différence*, kuʁɑ̃ *courant*, l apaʁɑ̃ːs *l'apparance*, aʁɑ̃ʒe *arranger*, ʒyʁe *jurer*, la faʁin *la farine*, kaʁɛse *caresser*, yn səʁiːz *une cerise*, œ̃ kaʁɔs *un carrosse*, yn ʃaʁɛt *une charrette*, l œʁɔp *l'Europe*.

302. ʁ *Initially* (Round the lips for ʁ before a rounded vowel) : ʁɑ, ʁɔ, ʁo, ʁu, ʁa, ʁɛ, ʁe, ʁi, ʁy, ʁø, ʁœ, ʁə, ʁɛ̃, ʁɑ̃, ʁɔ̃, ʁœ̃, ʁakɔmɔde *raccommoder*, ʁamase *ramasser*, ʁapid *rapide*, ʁa *rat*, ʁɔb *robe*, ʁɔ̃ːd *ronde*, ʁu *roue*, ʁuːʒ *rouge*, ʁezɔ̃ *raison*, ʁepete *répéter*, ʁido *rideau*, ʁjɛ̃ *rien*, ʁybɑ̃ *ruban*, ʁybi *rubis*, ʁy *rue*, ʁəfyze *refuser*, ʁwa *roi*.

303. ʁ *Following a Consonant Sound*—

(i) If the preceding consonant is voiceless the ʁ is generally only partially voiced. This is not usually marked in a phonetic transcription : pʀɑ, pʀɔ, pʀo, pʀu, pʀa, pʀɛ, pʀe, pʀi, etc. pʀatik *pratique*, pʀɛ *prêt*, pʀɛse *presser*, pʀezɑ̃te *présenter*, pʀepaʀe *préparer*, pʀesjø *précieux*, pʀie *prier*, pʀi *prix*, pʀɔfɔ̃ *profond*, pʀɔmnad *promenade*, pʀɔnɔ̃se *prononcer*, pʀœːv *preuve*, pʀɛ̃sipal *principal*, pʀəmje *premier*, pʀɔvɔke *provoquer*.

tʀɑ, tʀɔ, tʀo, tʀu, tʀa, tʀɛ, tʀe, tʀi, etc., tʀavaje *travailler*, tʀene *traîner*, tʀɛːz *treize*, tʀist *triste*, tʀo *trop*, tʀu *trou*, tʀuve *trouver*, tʀwa *trois*, tʀɑ̃ble *trembler*, tʀɑ̃ʃe *trancher*, tʀɑ̃pe *tremper*.

kʀɑ, kʀɔ, kʀo, kʀu, kʀa, kʀɛ, kʀe, kʀi, etc., kʀake *craquer*, kʀwa *croit*, kʀɛjɔ̃ *crayon*, kʀi *cri*, kʀɛːm *crème*, kʀɛ̃ːt *crainte*.

(ii) If the preceding consonant is voiced the ʀ is fully voiced : bʀɑ, bʀɔ, bʀo, bʀu, bʀa, bʀɛ, bʀe, bʀi, etc. bʀa *bras*, bʀaːv *brave*, bʀɛf *bref*, bʀize *briser*, bʀɔʃ *broche*, bʀɔde *broder*, bʀyle *brûler*, bʀəbi *brebis*, bʀɑ̃ːʃ *branche*, bʀœ̃ *brun*.

dʀɑ, dʀɔ, dʀo, dʀu, dʀa, dʀɛ, dʀe, dʀi, etc., dʀa *drap*, dʀapo *drapeau*, dʀwa *droit*, dʀoːl *drôle*, dʀy *dru*.

gʀɑ, gʀɔ, gʀo, gʀu, gʀa, gʀɛ, gʀe, gʀi, etc., gʀɑːs *grâce*, gʀɑ *gras*, gʀate *gratter*, gʀɔ̃de *gronder*, gʀoːs *grosse*, gʀɛːn *graine*, gʀɛ̃ *grain*, gʀɑ̃ *grand*.

304. ʀ *Finally, Preceded by a Vowel*—ʀ in this position is very weak : ɑːʀ, ɔːʀ, oːʀ, uːʀ, aːʀ, ɛːʀ, eːʀ, iːʀ, yːʀ, øːʀ, œːʀ, ɛ̃ːʀ, ɑ̃ːʀ, ɔ̃ːʀ, œ̃ːʀ, paːʀ *part*, taːʀ *tard*, ɑ̃ ʀtaːʀ *en retard*, pɔːʀ *port*, ɑ̃kɔːʀ *encore*, lə bɔːʀ *le bord*, o bɔːʀ də la mɛːʀ *au bord de la mer*, puːʀ *pour*, lə ʒuːʀ *le jour*, tuʒuːʀ *toujours*, puʀ tuʒuːʀ *pour toujours*, luːʀ *lourd*, vɛːʀ *verre*, pɛːʀ *père*, la manjɛːʀ *la manière*, nesesɛːʀ *nécessaire*, ʃɛːʀ *chère*, klɛːʀ *clair*, piːʀ *pire*, fiːʀ *firent*, liːʀ *lire*, diːʀ *dire*, ʀiːʀ *rire*, gʀɑ̃diːʀ *grandir*, myːʀ *mûr*, dyːʀ *dur*, pyːʀ *pur*, syːʀ *sûr*, la natyːʀ *la nature*, la kɔ̃fityːʀ *la confiture*, œ̃ myʀmyːʀ *un murmure*, lə kœːʀ *le cœur*, l œːʀ *l'heure*, la favœːʀ *la faveur*, œ̃ vɔlœːʀ *un voleur*, œ̃ mɑ̃tœːʀ *un menteur*, ma sœːʀ *ma sœur*, la pœːʀ *la peur*, la gʀɑ̃dœːʀ *la grandeur*, il plœːʀ *il pleure*.

305. ʁ *Finally, Preceded by a Consonant Sound—*

(i) If the preceding consonant is voiceless the ʁ is generally completely voiceless : ɑːpʁ̥ *âpre*, abatʁ̥ *abattre*, katʁ̥ *quatre*, fjakʁ̥ *fiacre*, kɔfʁ̥ *coffre*, pʁɛːtʁ̥ *prêtre*, mɛtʁ̥ *mettre*, lɛtʁ̥ *lettre*, oːtʁ̥ *autre*, ɑ̃ːkʁ̥ *encre*, sɑ̃ːtʁ̥ *centre*, kɔnɛːtʁ̥ *connaître*, lə noːtʁ̥ *le nôtre*.

(ii) If the preceding consonant is voiced the ʁ is often only partially voiced. It is not necessary to mark this in a phonetic transcription : tɛ̃ːbʁ *timbre*, sɔ̃ːbʁ *sombre*, atɑ̃ːdʁ *attendre*, pɛ̃ːdʁ *peindre*, ɛːgʁ *aigre*, ʃɑ̃ːbʁ *chambre*, aʁbʁ *arbre*.

306. Here it is convenient to refer to the pronunciation of words like the above, e.g. *quatre*, *autre*, *chambre*, *arbre*, etc., when they occur *medially* in a group. Note the following points :—

(i) When followed by a vowel the ʁ is fully voiced : la ʃɑ̃ːbʁ a kote *la chambre à côté*, nɔvɑ̃ːbʁ e desɑ̃ːbʁ *novembre et décembre*, lə poːvʁ ɔm *le pauvre homme*, a katʁ œːʁ *à quatre heures*, mɛtʁ yn lɛtʁ a la pɔst *mettre une lettre à la poste*, yn otʁ istwaːʁ *une autre histoire*, lə teɑːtʁ almɑ̃ *le théâtre allemand*, pʁɑ̃dʁ œ̃n oːtʁ *prendre un autre*, ɑ̃tɑ̃dʁ œ̃ bʁɥi *entendre un bruit*, vɔtʁ avi *votre avis*, l otʁ ɑ̃fɑ̃ *l'autre enfant*, mɑ̃bʁ aktif *membre actif*, l ilystʁ aktœːʁ *l'illustre acteur*.

(ii) When followed immediately by a consonant sound the orthographic *e* which ends such words is given a sound-value : ə :—yn ʃɑ̃bʁə ʃoːd *une chambre chaude*, lə povʁə bɔnɔm *le pauvre bonhomme*, katʁə paːʒ *quatre pages*, yn lɛtʁə d almaɲ *une lettre d'Allemagne*, yn otʁə fwa *une autre fois*, lə teɑːtʁə fʁɑ̃sɛ *le théâtre français*, pʁɑ̃dʁə lə te *prendre le thé*, ɑ̃tɑ̃dʁə lə bʁɥi dy vɑ̃ *entendre le bruit du vent*, vɔtʁə kɛstjɔ̃ *votre question*, l otʁə pɛʁsɔn *l'autre personne*, mɑ̃bʁə də l akademi *membre de l'Académie*, l œvʁə də ʁasin *l'œuvre de Racine*, l ilystʁə dɔktœːʁ *l'illustre docteur*.

(iii) In familiar conversation words of common use are pronounced without both ə and ʁ before a word beginning with a consonant : kat pa:ʒ *quatre pages*, dəpɥi kat ʒu:ʁ *depuis quatre jours*, lə pov bɔnɔm *le pauvre bonhomme*, mɛt d ɔtɛl *maître d'hôtel*, yn ot fwa *une autre fois*, s ātād di:ʁ *s'entendre dire*, i fo ɛt sa:ʒ *il faut être sage*, madam vɔt tā:t *madame votre tante*, pʁād lə te *prendre le thé*.

307. ʁ *Medially, Followed by a Consonant*—

If the consonant is voiceless, as in the examples given under (i) below, the ʁ is generally only partially voiced. In the examples given under (ii) the ʁ should be fully voiced.

N.B.—Pronounce *short* the vowel preceding ʁ followed by a consonant sound. (See § 419.)

(i) yn sɔʁt *une sorte*, la tɔʁʃ *la torche*, apɛʁsy *aperçu*, apɔʁte *apporter*, pɛʁsɔn *personne*, yn buʁs *une bourse*, la pɛʁt *la perte*, sɛʁtē *certain*, fɔʁse *forcer*, yn fuʁʃ *une fourche*, ʃɛʁʃe *chercher*, kuʁt *courte*, gaʁsɔ̃ *garçon*, kuvɛʁt *couverte*, debaʁke *débarquer*, la paʁti *la partie*, œ̃ paʁk *un parc*, yn avɛʁs *une averse*.

(ii) la baʁb *la barbe*, la fɛʁm *la ferme*, lə ʃaʁm *le charme*, la pɛʁl *la perle*, œ̃ bɛʁʒe *un berger*, ʃaʁʒe *charger*, lə ʃaʁbɔ̃ *le charbon*, la fɔʁm *la forme*, œ̃ ʃaʁlatā *un charlatan*, lə fɛʁmje *le fermier*, yn kɔʁd *une corde*, gaʁde *garder*, l ɛʁb *l'herbe*, la gɔʁʒ *la gorge*, l ɔʁlɔ:ʒ *l'horloge*, debɔʁde *déborder*, laʁʒ *large*, le laʁm *les larmes*, dɛʁnje *dernier*, ɔpsɛʁve *observer*, paʁdɔ̃ *pardon*, la sɔʁbɔn *la Sorbonne*.

308. ʁ *Followed by* ɥ—Practise words in which ʁ is followed by ɥ, first lengthening the ɥ (i.e. substituting y for it), then with the correct number of syllables : ʁyiso, ʁɥiso *ruisseau* ; ʁyine, ʁɥine *ruiner* ; fʁyi, fʁɥi *fruit* ; tʁyit, tʁɥit *truite* ; ʁyɛl, ʁɥɛl *ruelle*.

3. Uvular Rolled *r* (ʁ)

309. Description

1. The back of the tongue is raised to touch the uvula. The front of the tongue is depressed, the sides

raised, forming a rather wide channel down the centre of the tongue.

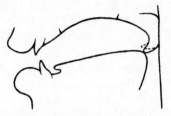

DIAGRAM 56—Uvular rolled *r* (ʀ).   (The raising of the *sides* of the tongue is not shown.)

2. The air passage is closed and opened two or three times at the point of articulation as the uvula vibrates up and down in the channel formed down the centre of the tongue.   This movement of the uvula can be distinctly seen.   The same movement takes place in gargling.

3. The sound is generally voiced.

Usage

310. Some French people use a ʀ, with one or two taps, in all positions, except perhaps finally after a vowel sound. Others think they always use ʀ. They probably *do* use it before and after consonant sounds and in emphatic speech.   In final positions after a vowel sound ʀ is not often heard in ordinary speech.

311. Many who normally use ʁ replace it by ʀ in emphatic speech.

Teaching Hints

312. Start from ʁ and use slightly more breath force. If this does not result in one or two taps of the uvula, move the position of the back of the tongue slightly : a little higher or lower, a little farther back or forward,

until you find a position where you can produce vibration of the uvula.

313. There should be no " scrapy " accompaniment to ʀ. Like r, it consists of one or two distinct little taps.

Exercises

314. For exercises in all positions see §§ 301–8 substituting ʀ for ʁ.

CHAPTER XV

NOTES ON THE FRENCH FRICATIVE CONSONANTS

315. Fricative consonants are made by narrowing the air-passage at some point to such an extent that friction is produced as the air passes through.

316. The chief fricative consonants in French are f, v, s, z, ʃ, ʒ.[1] They present no great difficulty to the English learner.

317. j, as a fricative consonant, is referred to in § 345.

318. The sound of the glottal fricative h in French is dealt with in §§ 332–7.

319. f, v. The place of articulation of f and v is the same as in English. The French sounds are pronounced with greater energy than the English ones.

320. v is generally fully voiced. (See §§ 328–30.)

321. s, z. In both English and French these sounds may be made with the tip of the tongue either raised or lowered. The difference in acoustic effect is not perceptible.

322. In the most usual variety of English s and z the tip and blade are raised to the teeth-ridge leaving a very narrow passage :

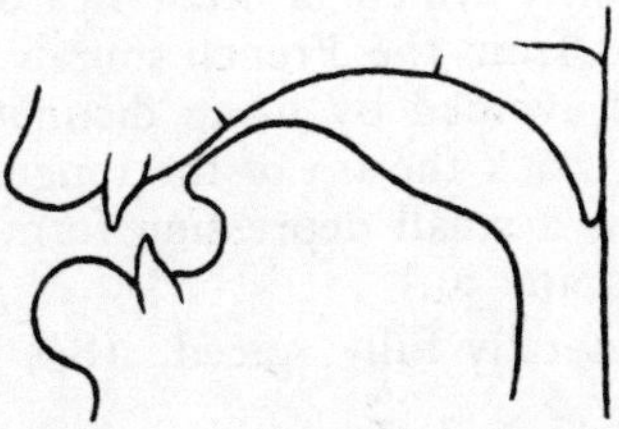

DIAGRAM 57—English s and z with the tip of the tongue raised.

[1] For ʀ see §§ 295–308.

323. In French the most usual variety of s and z is made with the tip of the tongue touching the lower teeth, the narrowing being between the blade and the teeth-ridge :

DIAGRAM 58—French s and z with the tip of the tongue lowered.

324. The English learner who articulates s and z with the tip raised need take no trouble to produce the French sounds with the tip of the tongue lowered. What is important is that he should make the French sounds with tense muscles of the tongue, with the tip of the tongue more advanced than for English s and z, and with a slightly greater narrowing of the air passage, if possible. The French sounds are clean-cut : there is about them none of the laxness of articulation common in the English varieties.

325. z is generally fully voiced. (See §§ 328–30.)

326. ʃ, ʒ. The place of articulation of ʃ and ʒ is about the same as for English ʃ and ʒ. The palatal (i.e. j-like) quality which is often heard in English ʃ and ʒ is absent from the French sounds. This palatal quality can be avoided by using distinct lip-rounding and by curling back the tip of the tongue very slightly so that there is a small depression formed behind the tip. (See diagram 59.)

327. ʒ is generally fully voiced. (See §§ 328–30.)

The Voicing of v, z, ʒ.

328. What has been said in §§ 256–9 about the voicing of b, d, g applies to v, z, ʒ.

329. When v, z, and ʒ occur in initial and final positions in French, the English learner often fails to voice them fully. This inability to use full voicing is especially noticeable in final positions. In intervocalic positions the voicing used by many English speakers sounds weak to a French ear.

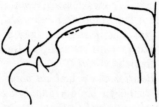

DIAGRAM 59—French ʃ and ʒ [1] (dotted line) compared with English ʃ and ʒ.

330. The following exercises should help the learner to produce fricative consonants with full, strong voicing :

1. Try to sing three or four notes up or down the musical scale on the sound z. If you allow the voicing to stop, the tune will also stop, since voiceless sounds cannot carry the tune. (Try to sing a tune on s. You will at once realize this.)

2. Alternate s with z making no pause between the sounds, and producing z with a strong "buzz" : s z s z

3. Fully voiced z in isolation.

4. zi, ze, zɛ, za, etc.

5. iz, ez, ɛz, az, etc.

6. f v f v

7. vi, ve, vɛ, va, etc.

8. iv, ev, ɛv, av, etc.

9. ʃ ʒ ʃ ʒ (with lip-rounding).

10. ʒi, ʒe, ʒɛ, ʒa, etc.

11. iʒ, eʒ, ɛʒ, aʒ, etc.

---

[1] Some French (and English) speakers lower the tip for ʃ and ʒ and articulate with the blade.

331. **Practice of Fricatives in French Words:**

(a) *In non-Final Positions:* fɛt sa *faites ça,* fɛtz atãsjõ *faites attention,* fɛrme la pɔrt *fermez la porte,* s i vu plɛ *s'il vous plaît,* sɛ̃pləmã *simplement,* siz ãfã *six enfants,* sɛt ʃã:br *sept chambres,* sɛ̃kãt su *cinquante sous,* s ɛt œ̃ ʃa *c'est un chat,* s ɛt œ̃ ʃjɛ̃ *c'est un chien,* ʃãte bjɛ̃ *Chantez bien,* vwasi *voici,* vwala *voilà,* vãdrədi *vendredi,* vuz ɛtz ã rta:r *vous êtes en retard,* vɛ̃tsɛ̃:k *vingt-cinq,* ʒã *Jean,* ʒystəmã *justement,* ʒãvje *janvier,* ʒamɛ *jamais,* ʒə vuz atã *je vous attends,* ʒə l e fini *je l'ai fini,* dissɛt *dix-sept,* dizɥit *dix-huit.*

(b) *In Final Position:* dy bœf *du bœuf,* ʒ e swaf *j'ai soif,* yn ta:s *une tasse,* yn œr dis *une heure dix,* truve yn plas *trouver une place,* la pɔʃ *la poche,* yn muʃ *une mouche,* turne a go:ʃ *tourner à gauche,* uvre la buʃ *ouvrez la bouche,* de vaʃ *des vaches,* tu le dimã:ʃ *tous les dimanches,* ʒə marʃ *je marche,* ɛl ɛ blã:ʃ *elle est blanche,* il ɛ riʃ *il est riche,* ʒə m lɛ:v *je me lève,* il ari:v *il arrive,* su la ʃɛ:z *sous la chaise,* yn bɛl ro:z *une belle rose,* sa m amy:z *ça m'amuse,* swasãt e õ:z *soixante et onze,* swasãt kɛ̃:z *soixante quinze,* yn mezõ frãsɛ:z *une maison française,* õ:z *onze,* du:z *douze,* trɛ:z *treize,* katɔrz *quatorze,* kɛ̃:z *quinze,* sɛ:z *seize,* ɛl ɛ parɛsø:z *elle est paresseuse,* de ry dãʒrø:z *des rues dangereuses,* yn ʒurne ãnɥijø:z *une journée ennuyeuse,* il ɛ ru:ʒ *il est rouge,* dy frɔma:ʒ *du fromage,* yn ɔrã:ʒ *une orange,* bõ vwaja:ʒ *bon voyage,* le baga:ʒ *les bagages,* s ɛt œ̃ sɛ̃:ʒ *c'est un singe,* syr la pla:ʒ *sur la plage,* lez ɔrɛ:j *les oreilles,* œ̃ ku d œ:j *un coup d'œil,* la fi:j *la fille,* lə sɔlɛ:j *le soleil,* lə trava:j *le travail,* œ̃ fotœ:j *un fauteuil.*

The sound of h

332. h is the weak fricative sound made as the air passes through the open glottis. The tongue is at the same time in position for the following vowel, e.g. hi *he,* hɑd *hard,* hu *who.*

333. The sound of *h* may be heard in certain French dialects, e.g. in that of Normandy, Brittany, Gascony, Lorraine. It is rarely heard in what may be called

standard French. Some French people use it in exclamations like *hé*, he:, *ha* hɑ:, *hola* hɔla, etc., and as an intensity device, e.g. *je le hais* ʒə lə ‖hɛ, *c'est une honte* s ɛt yn ‖hɔ̄:t. Some French people never use the sound of *h* at all, and it is never necessary to use it.

334. It is not sufficient, however, to know that the sound of *h* need not be pronounced. What is meant by *h* mute? *h* aspirate? *habile* abil is said to begin with *h* mute, *hauteur* otœ:r with *h* aspirate. In neither case is the *h* pronounced. Why, then, the use of these two terms?

335. *h* mute has no function at all. *h* aspirate, though, like *h* mute, it has no sound-value, plays the part of ruling out any possibility of liaison with the preceding word and of elision of the preceding vowel. One must say le otœ:r (and not lez otœ:r) *les hauteurs*, ɑ̃ o (and not ɑ̃n o) *en haut*, il ɛ arɖi (and not il ɛt arɖi) *il est hardi*, lə ʮit (and not l ʮit) *le huit*,[1] lə o (and not l o) *le haut*, etc.

The stress given to a syllable beginning with *h* aspirate must never include in its impulse the final consonant sound of the preceding word, no matter whether this word has a liaison form or not. *Avec haine* is avɛk ˈɛ:n [2] (or avɛk ‖ˀɛ:n or avɛk ‖hɛ:n) and not avɛ ˈkɛ:n. (In the case of stressed syllables beginning with a vowel—not with *h* aspirate—it is typical in unemphatic French to include in the stress the final consonant sound of the preceding word: *il aime* i ˈlɛ:m, *avec elle* avɛ ˈkɛl, *un homme* œ̃ ˈnɔm). *Par honte* is par ˈɔ̄:t [2] (or par ‖ˀɔ̄:t or par ‖hɔ̄:t) and not pa ˈrɔ̄:t. (Cf. *par an* pa ˈrɑ̃.)

336. Before *h* aspirate preceded by a word normally ending in a consonant sound and spelt with final *e*, e.g. yn *une*, sɛt *cette*, grɑ̃:d *grande*, this final *e* is often

---

[1] The *h* of *huit* is " mute " in compounds, and liaison is made before it : dizʮit *dix-huit*, vɛ̃tʮit *vingt-huit*.

[2] As in English *an egg* ən ˈɛg (not ə ˈnɛg) ; *for ever* fər ˈɛvə (not fə ˈrɛvə).

pronounced ə : ynə otœːr *une hauteur*, ynə ɛ *une haie*, sɛtə oːt mezõ *cette haute maison*, grãdə ɑːt *grande hâte*. In the case of some words, however, e.g. *faire*, *être*, it is more usual not to pronounce the final *e* before *h* aspirate. *Faire halte* is generally fɛr ˈalt (not fɛrə ˈalt, and not with the stress on ˈralt). *Être hors de soi* is generally ɛtr ˈɔːr də ˈswa. Some French speakers insert a weak glottal stop : yn ˀotœːr, fɛr ˀalt. The latter pronunciation is not recommended to English learners because of their tendency to use the glottal stop where its presence is not justified by French usage.

337. Words beginning with *h* aspirate are noted with a special mark in most dictionaries.

CHAPTER XVI

THE FRENCH SEMI-VOWELS OR VOWEL GLIDES

338. The French semi-vowels are j, ɥ, and w.

j

Description

339. For all practical purposes the semi-vowel j may be regarded as a rapid glide away from the vowel position of i to that of the following vowel, e.g. *fiacre* fjakṛ, *travailler* travaje. The vowel i is a syllabic sound. The semi-vowel j is too short to form a syllable.

340. The articulation of French j presents no difficulty to English learners ; it is like that of the semi-vowel j in English, heard in *yield* jild, *yellow* jɛlou, *yard* jɑd. No special exercises are therefore necessary.

Usage

341. j is often represented by the letter *i*, which also frequently represents the vowel i. The difficulty is to know when to use the semi-vowel and when to use the vowel.

342. As a general rule the letter *i* is pronounced j before a vowel sound :

1. When a single consonant sound precedes in the same syllable : *fièvre* fjɛːvr, *fier* fje (also fie), *bien* bjɛ̃, *pied* pje, *marier* marje, *premier* prəmje, *dernier* dɛrnje, *impression* ɛ̃prɛsjɔ̃, *tiède* tjɛd, *pion* pjɔ̃, *kiosque* kjɔsk, *pioche* pjɔʃ, *miel* mjɛl, *expier* ɛkspje.

2. When a vowel sound precedes : *travailler* travaje, *envoyer* ɑ̃vwaje, *cahier* kaje, *mouiller* muje.

343. After two consonant sounds in the same syllable

the letter *i* is generally pronounced i : *triangle* triɑ̃:gl,
triomphe triɔ̃:f, *brioche* briɔʃ, *grief* griɛf, *oublier* ublie,
plier plie, *encrier* ɑ̃krie, *bibliothèque* bibliɔtɛk, *tablier*
tablie.

344. The semi-vowel j is pronounced partially or
wholly without voice after a voiceless sound, e.g. pj̊e,
kj̊ɔsk.[1]

345. The semi-vowel j can occur only before a
vowel sound, since it is a glide from one vowel position
to another. What, then, is the sound (transcribed
phonetically with the symbol j) which closes a syllable,
final or non-final : *la fille* la fi:j, *le travail* lə trava:j,
le soleil lə sɔlɛ:j, *la bataille* la batɑ:j, *feuillton* fœjtɔ̃,
tressaillement trɛsajmɑ̃? In such positions j may be
pronounced in the following ways : (1) as a weak fricative
consonant, i.e. with the front of the tongue raised
higher than for the vowel i, so that friction is produced.[2]
(There is no separate symbol for j pronounced with
friction) ; (2) as a very short vowel, the tongue not
reaching the position where friction is made ; (the
sound then forms one syllable with the preceding
vowel) : trava:ĭ, trɛsaĭmɑ̃ ; (3) as a semi-vowel, a faint ə
being added : lə trava:jᵊ.

ɥ

Description

346. The semi-vowel ɥ may be regarded as a rapid
glide away from the vowel position of y to that of the
following vowel, e.g. *muet* mɥɛ, *nuage* nɥa:ʒ. The
vowel y is a syllabic sound ; the semi-vowel ɥ is too
short to form a syllable.

347. The articulation of ɥ should not be difficult to
English learners who can make the vowel y; and yet

---

[1] It is not necessary to use a diacritical mark or a special symbol
to remind the English learner of this. He uses a j of the same kind
in similar positions in English, e.g. *pew* is generally pj̊u, *Kew* is kj̊u.

[2] This fricative consonant is often heard instead of the semi-
vowel before the vowel i, e.g. *fouillis* fuji.

it is often badly pronounced, suggesting the tongue position of u rather than that of y. Practise yi, ye, yɛ, ya, etc. (two syllables). Then start again from the position of y, moving away from it immediately, so that there is no sound but the glide to the following vowel : ɥi, ɥe, ɥɛ, ɥa, etc. (one syllable).

Usage

348. Both ɥ and y are represented by the letter *u*. English people often find it difficult to know when to use the semi-vowel and when to use the vowel.

349. As a general rule *u* is pronounced ɥ before a vowel sound :

1. When a single consonant sound precedes in the same syllable : *tuer* tɥe (also tye), *juin* ʒɥɛ̃, *ruelle* rɥɛl, *écuelle* ekɥɛl, *lueur* lɥœːr, *luette* lɥɛt, *remuer* rəmɥe, *persuader* pɛrsɥade.

2. When the vowel i follows. In this case ɥ may be initial or preceded by one or more consonant sounds. It is generally pronounced with friction before i[1] : *huit* ɥit, *lui* lɥi, *pluie* plɥi, *fuir* fɥiːr, *cuivre* kɥiːvr, *puis* pɥi, *ruine* rɥin, *truite* trɥit, *fruit* frɥi, *bruit* brɥi, *druide* drɥid.

350. After two consonant sounds in the same syllable the letter *u* is generally pronounced y (unless the following vowel is i) : *cruauté* kryote, *cruel* kryɛl, *monstrueux* mõstryø, *influence* ɛ̃flyɑ̃ːs, *truelle* tryɛl.

w

Description

351. The semi-vowel **w** may be regarded as a rapid glide away from the vowel position of u to that of the following vowel, e.g. *oui* wi, *coin* kwɛ̃, *bois* bwɑ, *mouette*

---

[1] My colleague, Miss Coustenoble, tells me that there is no friction in ɥ before i in words beginning with *h* mute, e.g. *huile* ɥil, *huitre* ɥitr̩.

mwɛt, *avouer* avwe. The vowel u is syllabic. The semi-vowel w is too short to form a syllable.

352. The articulation of **w** in French gives no difficulty to English learners who can make the vowel u. French **w** is pronounced more energetically and with stronger lip-rounding than the semi-vowel **w** in English, heard in *weed* wid, *worn* wɔn, *one* wʌn.

Usage

353. Both **w** and **u** are represented by the letters *ou*. English people often find it difficult to know when to use the semi-vowel and when to use the vowel.

354. As a general rule *ou* is pronounced **w** before a vowel sound when a single consonant sound precedes in the same syllable : *fouet* fwɛ, *fouir* fwiːr, *douane* dwan, *douaire* dwɛːr, *jouer* ʒwe (also ʒue), *Chouan* ʃwã.

355. *ou* is pronounced **u** when more than one consonant sound precedes in the same syllable : *brouée* brue, *éblouir* ebluiːr, *prouesse* pruɛs, *grouiller* gruje, *clouer* klue, *trouée* true.

CHAPTER XVII

STRESS AND INTONATION

356. Stress is the speech effort made in pronouncing a syllable. Effort is, of course, expended on each syllable of a sound-group in connected speech ; but only those syllables which are pronounced with more energy than their neighbours are said to be *stressed*. The others are described as *unstressed*.

357. Stress is not a matter of force of exhalation only : it includes greater muscular activity of the organs of articulation, especially of the tongue and lips. There is probably also more tension in the larynx during the pronunciation of stressed syllables.

358. The result of stress is increased conspicuousness or prominence of the syllables upon which it is expended. Sometimes this prominence is only subjective : the speaker feels a syllable to be prominent, and to him it *is* prominent. The final syllable of a French sentence, for example, is often pronounced on such a low pitch that it is impossible to voice it. It is, in this case, not prominent at all to the hearer, though he may feel that it is important if he sees any outward signs of the speaker's effort which accompany it.

A. UNEMPHATIC STRESS

359. In English speech there is considerable difference between the amount of effort expended on the various syllables of a sound-group,[1] with the result that some syllables are " strong " and others " weak ". This unevenness of stress distribution is characteristic of English and also of German.

---

[1] A sound-group consists of the chain of speech sounds between two pauses.

360. In ᶦEnglish | the ᶦgreatest ᶦenergy | is ᶦused in proᶦnouncing ᶦwords of imᶦportant ᶦmeaning, | ᶦno matter ᶦwhat their poᶦsition in the ᶦsentence. || ᶦWords of ᶦsmall sigᶦnificance | are ᶦuttered with ᶦrelatively ᶦlittle exᶦpenditure of ᶦenergy. ||

361. The stress-marks in the preceding sentence show the words which the speaker regards as important in expressing his meaning ; they are placed before the stress-bearing syllable of each of those words. Notice that sometimes stress falls on a monosyllabic word, in some words on the first syllable, in others on the second. In some English words the main stress is on the third syllable : *diploᶦmatic, profesᶦsorial, inter-ᶦmediate, instruᶦmental, archiᶦtectural* ; in others the main stress is on the fourth syllable : *recommenᶦdation, humaniᶦtarian, experiᶦmental*. There is no fixed place for English stress, either in isolated words or in connected speech ; and yet there is a certain regularity in its occurrence which plays its part in producing the rhythm of English speech.

362. In French each syllable of a word pronounced unemphatically is uttered with about the same amount of energy, except the last, on which a slight increase of energy is expended. This final syllable is said to be stressed and bears a stress-mark ; non-final syllables are said to be unstressed, though they are not unstressed to exactly the same degree : *inutile* inyᶦtil, *phonétique* foneᶦtik, *Espagnol* ɛspaᶦɲol, *mademoiselle*, madmwaᶦzɛl, *grammatical* gramatiᶦkal, *généralement*, ʒeneralᶦmã, *administrateur* administraᶦtœːr.

363. It is possible to tap out the syllables of a French word regularly and with almost equal force on each. This regularity gives a staccato effect to French speech, which is quite impossible in English.

364. A short sentence in French may be regarded, from the point of view of stress, as a many-syllabled word : each non-final syllable is pronounced with fairly

even stress, the final syllable receiving slightly stronger
stress : *il va venir* il va vᵊniːr, *c'est inutile* s ɛt inyˈtil,
elle est malade ɛl ɛ maˈlad, *ça m'est égal* sa m ɛt eˈgal,
vous êtes en retard vuz ɛtz ã rˈtaːr, *il est sept heures* il ɛ
sɛt ˈœːr, *je n'en ai pas* ʒə n ãn e ˈpɑ.

365. If the sentence is divided into a number of
sense-groups,[1] each of these groups is like a many-
syllabled word, stress falling on the final syllable :
je suis rentré très tard ʒə sɥi rãˈtre | trɛ ˈtaːr ; ‖ *nous
l'avons vu chez elle* nu l avõ ˈvy | ʃez ˈɛl ; ‖ *je les ai vus
tout à l'heure* ʒə lez e ˈvy | tut a l ˈœːr ; ‖ *je comprends
bien ce que vous me dites* ʒə kõprã ˈbjɛ̃ | s kə vu m
ˈdit ; ‖ *il est arrivé en même temps que moi* il ɛt ariˈve |
ã mɛm tã k ˈmwa ; ‖ *nous arrivons bientôt chez nos amis*
nuz arivõ bjɛ̃ˈto | ʃe noz aˈmi ; ‖ *nous allons lire deux ou
trois pages du dernier chapitre* nuz alõ ˈliːr | dø u trwɑ
ˈpaːʒ | dy dɛrnje ʃaˈpitr̩ ; ‖ *nos parents de la campagne sont
chez nous depuis quinze jours* no parã d la kãˈpaɲ | sõ ʃe
ˈnu | dəpɥi kɛz ˈʒuːr ; ‖ *les enfants ferment leurs livres et*
les posent sur la table lez ãˈfã | fɛrm lœr ˈliːvr | et le
ˈpoːz | syr la ˈtabl ; ‖ *enfin, nous voici dans le quartier de
l'Hôtel de Ville* ãˈfɛ̃, | nu vwaˈsi | dã l karˈtje | d l ɔtɛl
də ˈvil ; ‖ *tous les matins la mère de Paul vient l'appeler
pour le réveiller et le faire lever* tu le maˈtɛ̃ | la mɛr də
ˈpɔl | vjɛ̃ l apˈle | pur lə revɛˈje | e lə fɛr ləˈve. ‖

366. Thus it may be said that stress in unemphatic
French has a fixed place : it falls on the final syllable
of a word in isolation and of a sense-group in connected
speech. This is not difficult to teach to English learners.

367. There is a tendency for the time intervals
between the stressed syllables of a sound-group to be
of the same length in English. In French also, stressed
syllables tend to recur at regular time intervals. But
the effect is far from being the same in the two languages.
In English strong syllables and long sounds may occur

---

[1] A sense-group consists of a group of words (sometimes of one
word only) having in itself a certain sense, not necessarily complete.

within the various sense-groups ; and the syllables which intervene are relatively very weak and short. In French strong syllables and long sounds occur only finally in each group ; and the intervening syllables are short, but they cannot be described as weak. Diagrammatically the difference in stress distribution may be represented thus :—

English : | . . . _ _ | . _ . _ . _ . . . | . _ . _ . |
. . _ . . . _ _ ||

French : | _ _ _ | _ _ _ _ | _ _ _ _ _ | _ _ _ _ ||

368. Intonation means the rise and fall of the pitch of the voice in speech. It is thus the musical element of speech. Stress and intonation cannot very well be studied apart, for they generally work together to make syllables prominent.

B. Unemphatic Intonation

369. With unemphatic stress goes unemphatic intonation. In French this intonation may be said to consist of a rising–falling " tune ". In some types of sentence both rising and falling elements are present ; in others the falling only ; in others the rising only.

1. Rising–falling Intonation

370. In a *short* unemphatic assertion of more than two syllables the typical intonation is a rising–falling one. This rise is made from a fairly low pitch and continues by very small musical intervals until the last syllable but one is reached.[1] Then follows a very low fall within the stressed syllable, sometimes so low that voicing is impossible :—

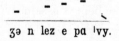

ʒə n lez e pɑ ˈvy.

[1] It is also very often possible, without being definitely emphatic, to give the top note to some syllable preceding the penultimate.

371. If the assertion has two syllables only, the pitch of the first is relatively high, that of the second low-falling :—

ʙ ɛ ˈvʀɛ.

372. If the assertion consists of one syllable only, the pitch is low-falling :—

ˈbɔ̃.

373. Try to say the short sentences given in § 364, and the following with the rising–falling intonation referred to above : *ça m'ennuie* sa m ɑ̃ˈnɥi, *il est vert* il ɛ ˈvɛːr, *il est midi* il ɛ miˈdi, *j'en suis content* ʒ ɑ̃ sɥi kɔ̃ˈtɑ̃, *il fait du vent* il fɛ dy ˈvɑ̃, *je ne comprends pas* ʒə n kɔ̃prɑ̃ ˈpɑ, *il vient de sortir* il vjɛ̃ d sɔr ˈtiːr, *nous les avons perdus* nu lez avɔ̃ pɛrˈdy.

374. In a *long* unemphatic assertion, the rising–falling intonation generally has another form. Instead of a continuous rise to a certain point followed by a continuous

fall, thus :   , the rising–

falling may be made thus :

or thus :   , etc.,

according to the number of sense-groups. The closer the meaning between two consecutive groups, the less deep the " valley " dividing them.

375. Here is given the intonation of some of the sentences from § 365 and of a few others. Notice that the stressed syllable of each non-final sense-group has the highest pitch of its group :—

◄········ Rising ········► ◄········ Falling ········►

```
        -    -    ▄          -
  -              |                 ╲
```

ʒə sɥi rɑ̃'tre | trɛ 'taːr ‖.
nu l avɔ̃ 'vy | ʃez 'ɛl ‖.
s ɛt a ko'te | d la 'gɑːr ‖.

◄········ Rising ········► ◄········ Falling ········►

```
  -   -   -   ▄        -   -
             |                 ╲
```

ʒə lez e 'vy | tut a l 'œːr ‖.
ʒə kɔ̃prɑ̃ 'bjɛ̃ | s kə vu m 'dit ‖.
kɑ̃t ɔ̃n a 'swaf | il fo 'bwaːr ‖.
il ɛ rɑ̃'tre | a ɔ̃z 'œːr ‖.
sɛt pətit 'fiːj | s apɛl ma'ri ‖.
nu l avɔ̃ 'vy | ʃe mɔ̃ 'pɛːr ‖.
s ɛt yn pətit mezɔ̃ 'blɑ̃ːʃ | prɛ d l e'kɔl ‖.

◄········ Rising ········► ◄········ Falling ········►

```
        ▄                -    -              -
  -   --       |    -   -          |    -   -
                                              ╲
```

nuz alɔ̃ 'liːr | dø u trwɑ 'pɑːʒ | dy dɛrnje ʃa'pitr̩ ‖.
lez a'bɛːj | abit yn ɛspɛs də me'zɔ̃ | k ɔ̃n apɛl yn 'ryʃ ‖.
no parɑ̃ d la kɑ̃'paɲ | sɔ̃ ʃe 'nu | dəpɥi kɛ̃z 'ʒuːr ‖.
a pa'ri | ɔ̃ pø s amy'ze | fasil'mɑ̃ ‖.

◄········ Rising ········► ◄········ Falling ········►

```
      -   -                       -   -              -   -
  -           |    -   -     |              |             ╲
```

lez ɑ̃'fɑ̃ | fɛrm lœr 'liːvr | e le 'pɔːz | syr la 'tabl ‖.

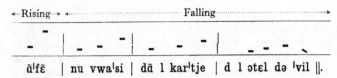

ã|fɛ̃ | nu vwa|si | dã l kar|tje | d l ɔtɛl də |vil ‖.

376. Expressions of small significance, like *monsieur*, *madame*, *dit-il*, etc., appended to assertions, have a low level or slightly falling intonation :—

il ɛt ɔ̃z |œːr, məsjø.

,, ,, ,, ,, madam.

,, ,, ,, ,, dit il.

,, ,, ,, ,, ma ptit.

il fɛ ɖy |vã oʒərdɥi.

,, ,, ,, ,, sə matɛ̃.

vuz ɛtz ã r|taːr, madmwazɛl.

2. Falling Intonation

377. A falling intonation

is the typical intonation of

(*a*) Questions [1] beginning with a specific interrogative word : *Où allez-vous?* u ale |vu? *Qu'allez-vous faire?* k ale vu |fɛːr? *Quel âge avez-vous?* kɛl ɑːʒ ave |vu? *Qu'est-ce que vous avez là?* k ɛ s kə vuz ave |la? *Quelle heure est-il?* kɛl œːr ɛt |il? *Comment vous appelez-vous?* kɔmã vuz aple |vu? *Pourquoi avez-vous fait ça?* purkwa ave vu fɛ |sa?

(*b*) Commands [1] and Requests : *Prenez vos livres*

---

[1] The rising–falling intonation is also possible, but it is not the typical intonation.

prəne vo ᴵliːvr. *Rangez vos affaires* rɑ̃ʒe voz aᴵfɛːr.
Mets-le dans la boîte mɛ lə dɑ̃ la ᴵbwat. *Tenez-vous droit*
təne vu ᴵdrwɑ. *Parlez plus haut* parle ply ᴵo. *Ecoutez-
moi bien* ekute mwa ᴵbjɛ̃. *Ne lisez pas si vite.* nə lize pɑ
si ᴵvit. *Viens jouer avec moi* vjɛ̃ ʒue avɛk ᴵmwa. *Va
chercher ton chapeau* va ʃɛrʃe tɔ̃ ʃaᴵpo.

378. In *long* sentences of the type requiring the falling
intonation the fall has a different form.   Instead of a

continuous fall, thus :   the fall may

be made thus :

or   etc., according

to the number of sense-groups.   The pitch of the
last syllable of each non-final sense-group is raised :—

kɔmɑ̃ dit ɔ̃ ᴵsa | ɑ̃ frɑ̃ᴵsɛ? [1] ||
ki vuz a ᴵdi | d vənir iᴵsi? ||
u ɛt vu alᴵe | s maᴵtɛ̃? ||
k ɛ s kə vuz ave ᴵvy | sɛt apremiᴵdi? ||
dit mwa purᴵkwa | vuz i ɛtz aᴵle. ||

379. Expressions of small significance, like *monsieur*,
madame, *demanda-t-il*, etc., appended to sentences

---

[1] The last sense-groups in these examples may also have the
rising–falling intonation :

The use of this necessitates a greater musical interval between
the groups, and therefore divides the ideas of the groups more
than the intonation given above.

pronounced with a falling intonation, have a low level
or slightly falling pitch, as after assertions. (See § 376.)

3. Rising Intonation

380. A rising intonation

is the typical intonation of (*a*) an unfinished assertion
(see examples § 375), (*b*) questions which may be
answered by " yes " or " no " : *Est-ce que vous le
comprenez?* ɛ s kə vu l kɔ̃prə'ne? *L'avez-vous trouvé?*
l ave vu tru've? *C'est intéressant?* s ɛt ɛ̃tɛrɛ'sɑ̃? *Vous
n'aimez pas ça?* vu n ɛme pɑ 'sa? *Vous avez remarqué?*
vuz ave rmar'ke?

381. In *long* groups requiring a rising intonation the
rise may have a different form. Instead of a continuous

rise   the rise may be

made thus :   or thus :

etc., according to the

number of sense-groups. The depth of the " valleys "
depends on the closeness of meaning existing between
adjacent groups.

ave vu 'ly | sɛt is'twa:r? |
kɔnɛse 'vu | s pei 'si? |
ave vuz aʃ'te | tu se 'li:vr? |

K

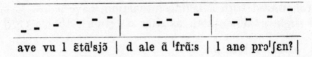

ave vu l ɛ̃tɑ̃ˈsjɔ̃ | d ale ɑ̃ ˈfrɑ̃ːs | l ane prɔˈʃɛn? |

382. The intonation of expressions appended to groups which have a rising intonation also rises :—

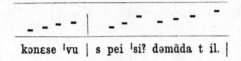

kɔnɛse ˈvu | s pei ˈsi? dəmɑ̃da t il. |

C. Emphasis

383. Emphasis, or special prominence, is used when a speaker wants either to *intensify* the meaning of certain words, e.g. " It's a *marvellous* improvement " ; " a *disgusting* sight " ; " *perfectly* charming " ; " a *frantic* effort " ; or to express a *contrast* of some kind, e.g. " This is a DIFFERENT one " (DIFFERENT offering a contrast to " same "), " He's coming NEXT week " (NEXT offering a contrast to " this "). " It had a TREMENDOUS effect " (contrast with " little " or " no "), " It was TRUE " (contrast with " false ").

384. The first kind of emphasis may be called *emphasis for intensity*. It is indicated by ‖ in this book. The second kind may be called *emphasis for contrast*. It is indicated by ⫽. We shall take each kind in turn and explain briefly the different ways by which each is expressed.

1. Emphasis for Intensity

385. The most important way of intensifying the meaning of a word is to increase the amount of energy used in pronouncing the appropriate syllable of that word.

386. In English the appropriate syllable is that which normally bears stress : *a pre‖posterous ˈstatement, a*

*ri*ǁ*diculous* ǀ*price, a tre*ǁ*mendous* ǀ*force, a mi*ǁ*raculous es*ǀ*cape,* ǁ*perfectly* ǁ*charming,* ǁ*full to the* ǀ*brim.*

387. In French the effect of this extra energy is tremendously enhanced because it is expended on some syllable other than the normal. The normal stress may be, and generally is, retained.

Place of Stress for Intensity in French

388. Monosyllabic words have their stress reinforced : *tout est fini* ǁtut ε fiǀni, *pas du tout,* ǁpɑ dy ǀtu, *c'est très difficile* s ε ǁtrɛ difiǀsil, *Quel sale temps* ! kɛl ǁsal ǀtɑ̃ ! *de tout mon cœur* də ǁtu mɔ̃ ǀkœːr, *c'est la seule chose qui me plaise* s ε la ǁsœl ʃoz ki m ǀplɛːz, *Faites bien attention* fɛt ǁbjɛ̃n atɑ̃sǀjɔ̃, *c'est un fou* s ɛt œ̃ ǁfu, *il ne comprend rien* il nə kɔ̃prɑ̃ ǁrjɛ̃.

389. In intensified words of more than one syllable a strong stress [1] is placed generally on the first syllable beginning with a consonant [2] : *c'est superbe,* s ε ǁsyǀpɛrb, *je ne l'ai jamais vu* ʒə n l e ǁʒamɛ ǀvy, *personne n'est venu* ǁpɛrsɔn n ε ǀvny, *c'est une charmante petite maison* s ɛt yn ǁʃarmɑ̃t pətit meǀzɔ̃, *c'est parfaitement inutile* s ε ǁparfɛtmɑ̃ inyǀtil, *ils sont toujours les mêmes* il sɔ̃ ǁtuʒur le ǀmɛːm, *il était enchanté* il etɛt ɑ̃ǁʃɑ̃ǀte, *c'est la même personne que j'ai vue hier* s ε la ǁmɛːm pɛrsɔn kə ʒ e vy ǀjɛːr, *vous avez parfaitement raison* vuz ave ǁparfɛtmɑ̃ reǀzɔ̃, *il était affreusement laid* il etɛt aǁfrøːzmɑ̃ ǀlɛ, *ça m'a énormément intéressé* sa m a eǁnɔrmemɑ̃ ɛ̃terɛǀse, *il l'a fait justement pour m'agacer* il l a fɛ ǁʒystəmɑ̃ pur m agaǀse.

Influence of Intensive Stress on Intonation

(a) On the Rising-falling Intonation—

390. If intensive stress falls on the final or penultimate syllable of a group there is no change in the position of

---

[1] Often called *shifted,* though there is no shifting of stress.

[2] It is possible also to place it on the first syllable, even if it begins with a vowel, but this is not as a rule recommended to the English learner, except in the case of commands. (See § 392.)

the highest pitch ; it is on the penultimate syllable, e.g.
c'est un fou s ɛt œ̃ ‖fu, *il ne comprend rien* il nə kɔ̃prɑ̃
‖rjɛ̃, *c'est un méchant* s ɛt œ̃ ‖me‖ʃɑ̃, *c'est excellent* s ɛt
ɛk‖sɛ‖lɑ̃, *c'est superbe* s ɛ ‖sy‖pɛrb, *elle devient tout rouge*
ɛl dəvjɛ̃ ‖tu ‖ru:ʒ.

391. If the intensified syllable occurs elsewhere in
the sentence the intonation form is different, since the
prominence of the highest pitch is given to the intensified
syllable, no matter what its position :

s ɛt yn ‖ʃarmɑ̃t pətit me‖zɔ̃.

s ɛ ‖trɛ difi‖sil.

s ɛ la ‖sœl ʃoz ki m ‖plɛ:z.

ʒə n l e ‖ʒamɛ ‖vy.

s ɛt ɛ̃‖pɔsib də l ‖fɛ:r.

s ɛ ‖parfɛtmɑ̃ iny‖til.

il etɛt a‖frø:zmɑ̃ ‖lɛ.

sa m a e‖nɔrmemɑ̃ ɛ̃terɛ‖se.

il l a fɛ ‖ʒystəmɑ̃ pur m aga‖se.

‖pɛrsɔn nə puvɛ l kɔ̃‖prɑ̃:dr.

‖tut ɛ fi‖ni.

‖rjɛ̃ nə lɥi ‖rɛst.

‖ply rjɛ̃ n ‖pɑ:s.

(b) On the Falling Intonation—

392. The meaning of questions beginning with a
specific interrogative word, of commands and requests
is generally intensified by increasing the stress in
pronouncing the specific interrogative word in the case

of the questions, and the verb in the case of commands
and requests. When these words occur initially, as
they generally do, there is no change in the position of
the highest pitch. Commands, even if they begin with
a vowel, usually have the highest pitch on the first
syllable :

‖ki a fɛ ¹sa?
‖finise vo ¹ʒø.
‖fɛrme la ¹pɔrt.
‖ale vuz ¹ɑ̃.
‖atɑ̃de ¹mwa.
‖ɑ̃lve se ¹liːvr.

If the question or command word is not initial, the
preceding syllable (or syllables) is generally on a low
pitch, so that the important syllable may stand out
prominently :

də ‖ki parle ¹vu?
avɛk ‖kwa ɛ s k ɔ̃ fɛ ¹sa?
nə ‖puse pɑ kɔm ¹sa.

(c) On the Rising Intonation—

393. (i) In the rising part of the rising–falling
intonation. The rise may be made in the normal way,
i.e. continuously. Note the level pitch of the final
syllable :

il sɔ̃ ‖trɛ ¹fjɛːr | də lœrz ɑ̃¹fɑ̃ ‖.
il etɛt ɑ̃‖ʃɑ̃¹te | d le ¹vwaːr ‖.

ilz ɔ̃ ‖bjɛ̃ travaˡje | pur lə fiˡniːr ‖.
s etɛt ɛ̃‖pɔsib də l ˡfɛːr | avɑ̃ lœ̈ˡdi ‖.

It is more effective, however, when there are syllables between the intensified and final ones (as in the last two examples) to give a high pitch to the intensified syllable and lower that of the syllables between it and the final one. The result is greater prominence of the intensified syllable :

ilz ɔ̃ ‖bjɛ̃ travaˡje | . . . . .
s ɛt ɛ̃‖pɔsib də l ˡfɛːr | . . . . .
ɛl etɛ ‖dezɔˡle | də l avwar pɛrˡdy ‖.
ʒə sre ɑ̃‖ʃɑ̃te d vu ˡvwaːr | dəmɛ̃ maˡtɛ̃ ‖.

394. (ii) In questions that may be answered by " yes " or " no ". If the interrogative element is emphasized, the first word (i.e. the verb) has a high pitch. Syllables between this and the final one have a falling intonation. The final syllable has a high level

pitch :   The effect of the fall

preceding the rise is to throw both first and last syllables into greater relief and thus produce a stronger impression of interrogation, curiosity, or surprise :

‖ɛ s kə vu l ave truˡve?
‖vɔ̃t il suvɑ̃ ɑ̃n ɑ̃gləˡtɛːr?
‖save vu purkwa il nə sɔ̃ paz iˡsi?
‖ɛ s kə vu l ave vy ɑ̃ ˡfrɑ̃ːs?

395. If it is desired to give prominence to some medial word, the final syllable of this word has the lowest pitch instead of the penultimate syllable :—

‖ɛ s kə vu l ave ˈvy ɑ̃ ˈfrɑ̃ːs?

‖ɛ ty kõˈtɑ̃ d tõn aprɛmiˈdi?

‖ɛ s kə pɛrˈsɔn na ete ɑ̃vwaˈje?

‖võt il suˈvɑ̃ ɑ̃n ɑ̃gləˈtɛːr?

‖save vu purˈkwa il nə sõ paz iˈsi?

396. The main factor in expressing intensity of meaning is, then, the use of extra stress. Often, as we have seen, there is also a modification of the intonation pattern which gives to the intensified syllable a pitch prominence it would not have in unemphatic speech.

397. Other factors (which operate also in English), such as a widening or narrowing of the range of intonation, length,[1] repetition, change of word order, addition of words, facial expression and gesture, etc., are also often present and add to the effect of intensity.

2. Emphasis for Contrast

398. Emphasis for contrast is expressed both in English and in French mainly by a sudden change in the *pitch* of the emphasized word. In both languages it is the *normally* stressed syllable which is affected. There may also be a reinforcement of the stress in pronouncing this syllable, but this is not essential.

399. The intonation proceeds normally until the emphasized syllable is reached. Then there is a sudden fall to a low pitch. If unstressed syllables follow, their pitch is low.

[1] See §§ 423, 424.

400. *Emphasis for Contrast in a Group Pronounced with the Rising–falling Intonation*—The rising–falling

intonation 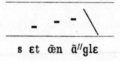 has the following

forms according to the position of the emphasized syllable :

(1) When the *final* word is emphasized for contrast, as in *c'est un* ANGLAIS s ɛt œn ɑ̃‖glɛ, the final syllable of this word falls from a high pitch to a very low one. The height depends on the strength of the contradiction :

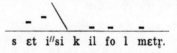

s ɛt œn ɑ̃‖glɛ

Other examples : *c'est* DIFFICILE s ɛ difi‖sil, *il est* CHARMANT il ɛ ʃar‖mɑ̃, *il était à* LONDRES il etɛt a ‖lɔ̃:dr, *nous l'avons* VENDU nu l avɔ̃ vɑ̃‖dy, *je trouve qu'elle est* GENTILLE ʒə truv k ɛl ɛ ʒɑ̃‖ti:j, *il faut aller par* ICI il fot ale par i‖si, *elle est* PARESSEUSE ɛl ɛ parɛ‖sø:z.

(2) When a *medial* word is emphasized for contrast the fall takes place in pronouncing the final syllable of the word :

s ɛt i‖si k il fo l mɛtr̩.

Other examples : *elle était* CHARMÉ *de nous voir*, ɛl etɛ ʃar‖me d nu vwa:r, *c'était à* PARIS *que nous l'avons vu* s etɛt a pa‖ri k nu l avɔ̃ vy, *c'est la* MÊME *personne* s ɛ la ‖mɛ:m pɛrsɔn, *il a fait* BEAU *hier* il a fɛ ‖bo jɛ:r, *c'est* VOUS *qui devez le faire* s ɛ ‖vu ki dve l fɛ:r, *c'est* MAL *de l'abîmer* s ɛ ‖mal də l abime, *en voilà une horreur !* ɑ̃ vwa‖la yn ɔrrœ:r !

(3) When the *initial* syllable is emphasized for contrast the fall takes place in pronouncing this syllable. In

the following examples the first word really forms a
sense-group in itself : ·

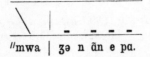

*//*mwa | ʒə n ãn e pɑ.

Other examples : ÇA *c'est bien fait //*sa | s ɛ bjɛ̃ fɛ,
NOUS *nous le comprenons //*nu | nu l kɔ̃prənɔ̃, MOI *j'irai à
Londres //*mwa | ʒ ire a lɔ̃:dr.

**401. Emphasis for Contrast in a Group Pronounced
with the Falling Intonation**—The falling intonation

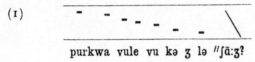 has the following forms according

to the position of the emphasized syllable :

(1)

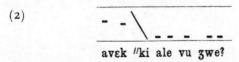

purkwa vule vu kə ʒ lə *//*ʃã:ʒ?

Other examples : *Qu'est-ce que vous allez faire*
AUJOURD'HUI? k ɛ s kə vuz ale fɛr oʒɔr*//*dɥi? *Pourquoi
veut-il le mettre* ICI? purkwa vøt il lə mɛtr i*//*si? *Mets-le
dans la* BOÎTE mɛ lə dã la *//*bwat.

(2)

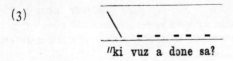

avɛk *//*ki ale vu ʒwe?

Other examples : *Depuis* QUAND *est-il à Londres?*
dəpɥi *//*kã ɛt il a lɔ̃:dr? POURQUOI *l'avez-vous fait?*
pur*//*kwa l ave vu fɛ? LAQUELLE *allez-vous voir?* la*//*kɛl
ale vu vwa:r?

(3)

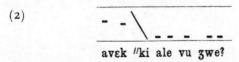

*//*ki vuz a dɔne sa?

Other examples : où *l'avez-vous trouvé?* *ᴵᴵu l ave vu truve?* QUAND *est-ce qu'il arrive* ᴵᴵkɑ̃ ɛ s k il ari:v? D'où *est-ce qu'elle vient?* d ᴵᴵu ɛ s k ɛl vjɛ̃?

402. *Emphasis for Contrast in a Group Pronounced with the Rising Intonation*—The rising intonation

has the following forms according to the position of the emphasized syllable :

(1)

ɛ s k il vuz a kɔ̃ᴵᴵpri?

or

Other examples : *Voulez-vous que je le* CHANGE? vule vu kə ʒə l ᴵᴵʃɑ̃:ʒ? *Est-ce que vous connaissez* MADAME? ɛ s kə vu kɔnɛse maᴵᴵdam?

(2)

ɛ s kə ᴵᴵvu lez ave vy?

or

Other examples : *Est-ce que monsieur* DUNOIS *le sait?* ɛ s kə məsjø dyᴵᴵnwa lə se? *Est-ce que vous* PARTEZ *demain?* ɛ s kə vu parᴵᴵte dəmɛ̃? *Est-ce que* MADAME *est ici?* ɛ s kə maᴵᴵdam ɛt isi?

(3) It is possible to say PART-*il demain?* JOUE-*t-il quelquefois?* etc., and the intonation would be—

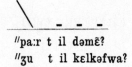

//paːr t il dəmɛ̃?
//ʒu   t il kɛlkəfwa?

But the normal way of asking such questions is with *Est-ce que*, in which case the emphasized word occurs medially, as under (2).

403. Intonation is the main factor in expressing contrast. Other factors are often present, e.g. extra stress, enlargement of the construction of the sentence, change of word order.

CHAPTER XVIII

LENGTH

404. It is possible with an instrument to measure a great number of degrees of length ; the ear can often distinguish five or six degrees ; but, luckily for the learner, there is no language in which so many as five or six degrees are significant or even very important.

405. In French, length is significant only to a very small extent. (See § 417 (iii).) Yet it is important that the English learner should know something about the length of sounds in French ; for if English habits of length are carried over to French, the result does not make for ready intelligibility.

406. Length in French, as in many other languages, is very closely connected with stress. In French, normal stress falls on the final syllable of each word pronounced in isolation, and on the final syllable of each sense-group. In this chapter it is proposed to examine the variations in the lengths of vowels in these final syllables, and also to examine in what way emphasis affects vowel length. Vowels in unstressed syllables, though by no means invariable in length, may for all practical purposes be considered short. (See § 421.) Consonant length is treated very briefly in §§ 428–34.

407. In recording length, even with elaborate detail, one can show only an approximation to actual facts. Some writers record three degrees of length : long, marked by : placed after the symbol for the sound lengthened ; short, unmarked ; half-long, marked · and used in unstressed syllables only. In this book the latter mark is dispensed with, and the number of degrees recorded reduced to two : long and short.

This simplifies the transcription considerably, without involving the sacrifice of anything of great importance.

I. Length of Vowels in Final, Normally Stressed Syllables

(a) Open Syllables

408. *Rule* : Vowel sounds in final, stressed open syllables are *short* : di *dit*, midi *midi*, te *thé*, dɔne *donner*, lə lɛ *le lait*, la pɛ *la paix*, il ɛ prɛ *il est prêt*, lə sɔlda *le soldat*, lə vwala *le voilà*, la bɑ *là-bas*, ʒə n sɛ pɑ *je ne sais pas*, tɑ̃to *tantôt*, bo *beau*, tut o bu *tout au bout*, partu *partout*, lə biʒu *le bijou*, s ɛt ɑ̃tɑ̃dy *c'est entendu*, presjø *précieux*, mulɛ̃ *moulin*, ɑ̃n atɑ̃dɑ̃ *en attendant*, syr lə pɔ̃ *sur le pont*, œ̃ a œ̃ *un à un*, sə matɛ̃ | ʒə n e pɑ l tɑ̃ | d ale o byro *ce matin je n'ai pas le temps d'aller au bureau*.

409. *Exceptions*

(i) Exceptions occur in Swiss and Belgian French, final vowels of feminine words ending in orthographic *e* being lengthened : œ̃n ami *un ami*, yn ami: *une amie* ; l avi *l'avis*, la vi: *la vie* ; il ɛ vny *il est venu*, ɛl ɛ vny: *elle est venue* ; il ɛt arive *il est arrivé*, ɛl ɛt arive: *elle est arrivée*. It is quite unnecessary for English learners to make this difference. As a rule, French speakers are prejudiced by the spelling when they profess to lengthen the vowel in the feminine form of such words in ordinary conversation. In reality they probably make no difference between the pronunciation of masculine and feminine forms, except in reading poetry.

(ii) The final vowel of an exclamation is lengthened : e: ! *He* ! ɑ: ! *Ah* ! The vowel of *mais* is often lengthened before a pause. *Oui* and *non*, pronounced in a very doubtful way, often have long vowels.

Mistakes of English Learners

410. The above rule is often broken by English speakers ; for in English the vowel in a final stressed open syllable is *long*, the length being often accompanied

by a movement of the position of the tongue and lower jaw, so that a diphthong is produced. Pronounce the following sentences aloud. You will find that the vowels in the final stressed words are long, and in the case of *day* and *go* they are diphthongized ¹ : *I ˈcan't find the ˈkey. He's ˈbought a ˈnew ˈcar. She's ˈcoming to-ˈday. I ˈdon't know ˈwhat to ˈdo. It's ˈmade of ˈfur. That's ˈall I ˈsaw. I ˈcan't ˈgo.* It is for this reason that an Englishman speaking French is tempted to say : ‖kɛs kə vuz ave ˈdiː? for ‖kɛs kə vuz ave ˈdi? ‖paː dy ˈtuː for ‖pa dy ˈtu; ‖kɛs kə ˈseɪ? for ‖kɛs kə ˈs ɛ? k il ɛ ˈbou! for k il ɛ ˈbo !

(b) Closed Syllables

411. *Rule* 1 — The four nasalized vowels, together with o, ø, and ɑ (when not preceded by w), are *long* in final stressed syllables closed by one or two consonant sounds.   The nature of the closing consonant is immaterial : pɛ̃ːtr̥ *peintre*, sɛ̃ːʒ *singe*, sɛ̃ːt *sainte*, lɑ̃ːp *lampe*, frɑ̃ːs *France*, sɑ̃ːbl *semble*, mɔ̃ːd *monde*, ɔ̃ːbr *ombre*, prɔfɔ̃ːd *profonde*, œ̃ːbl *humble*, koːt *côte*, foːs *fausse*, presjøːz *précieuse*, nøːtr̥ *neutre*, pɑːl *pâle*, tɑːs *tasse*, tɑːʃ *tâche*. But frwɑd *froide*, etrwɑt *étroite*.

Mistakes of English Learners

412. English learners observe the above rule without any difficulty, except perhaps in those words where the vowel is followed by a voiceless consonant : sɛ̃ːt, frɑ̃ːs, koːt, tɑːʃ, tɑːs, etc.   The tendency in such words is to make the vowel too short.   Some have a difficulty in saying drwɑt, frwɑd, etc., with a short ɑ.

413. *Rule* 2—All vowels in final stressed syllables are long if the closing consonant is r, v, vr, z, ʒ, or j ² : finiːr *finir*, liːr *lire*, kɥiːr *cuir*, pɛːr *père*, kɔlɛːr *colère*, tɛːr *terre*, dɛrjɛːr *derrière*, taːr *tard*, avwaːr *avoir*, istwaːr *histoire*, ɑ̃kɔːr *encore*, dəɔːr *dehors*, alɔːr *alors*, tuʒuːr

---

¹ The vowels of *key* and *do* are also diphthongized by many speakers.
² See also § 417 (ii).

toujours, luːr *lourd*, myːr *mur*, pœːr *peur*, sœːr *sœur*, elɛːv *élève*, flœːv *fleuve*, uːvr *ouvre*, liːvr *livre*, ʃɛːvr *chèvre*, biːz *bise*, səriːz *cerise*, trɛːz *treize*, duːz *douze*, ɔ̃ːz *onze*, tiːʒ *tige*, ɛːʒ *ai-je?* sovaːʒ *sauvage*, alɔ̃ːʒ *allonge*, fiːj *fille*, sɔlɛːj *soleil*, travaːj *travaille*, fotœːj *fauteuil*.

414. *Exception*—Many Parisians and others do not lengthen the vowel preceding j.

Mistakes of English Learners

415. The above rule is not difficult to observe, since in English the consonant sounds v and z have a lengthening effect on the preceding vowel. Compare the length of the vowels in *leaf* and *leave*, *fife* and *five*, *niece* and *knees*, *ice* and *eyes*. ʒ and r do not occur in absolutely final positions in English ; but the English student has no difficulty in lengthening the vowel preceding these sounds.

416. *Rule 3*—In cases not included in the previous rules (i.e. where a vowel other than ɛ̃, ɑ̃, ɔ̃, œ̃, o, ø, ɑ occurs in a stressed final syllable closed by one of the non-lengthening consonants : p, t, k, b,[1] d,[1] g,[1] m, n, ɲ, l) there is no fixed rule, but the vowel is generally short (most of the exceptions are in regard to ɛ) : vit *vite*, vid[2] *vide*, diɲ *digne*, il *île*, din *dîne*, pip *pipe*, vil *ville*, riʃ *riche*, pyblik *public*, sɑ̃tim *centime*, ytil *utile*, sɛl *sel*, sɛt *sept*, bɛk *bec*, sɛʃ *sèche*, prɔʃɛn *prochaine*, sal *salle*, fam *femme*, vaʃ *vache*, ras *race*, rad[2] *rade*, silab[2] *syllabe*, prɔmnad[2] *promenade*, pɔm *pomme*, pɔʃ *poche*, sɔl *sol*, dɔt *dot*, glɔb[2] *globe*, sɛ̃bɔl *symbole*, parɔl *parole*, kɔmɔd[2] *commode*, analɔg[2] *analogue*, sup *soupe*, buʃ *bouche*, dus *douce*, pul *poule*, lyn *lune*, nyl *nul*, ryd[2] *rude*, okyn *aucune*, minyt *minute*, ʒœn *jeune*, sœl *seul*.

417. *Exceptions*

(i) Many Swiss lengthen the a in the feminine ending -*ale* : nasjonaːl *nationale*, matinaːl *matinale*, l ɔpaːl *l'opale*,

---

[1] See also § 417 (ii).
[2] See exceptions, §§417 (ii).

mynisipaːl *municipale*. In the masculine ending -*al* the vowel is short : nasjɔnal *national*, etc.

(ii) There is a growing tendency to regard b, d, and g [1] as lengthening consonants. So common is this tendency that b, d, and g might be added to the list of lengthening consonants given in § 413. The lengthening takes place especially after a [2] and ɔ, but may be heard also after other vowels : malaːd *malade*, raːd *rade*, baːg bague, glɔːb *globe*, katalɔːg *catalogue*, viːd *vide*, etyːd *étude*. The a of the termination -*able* is also lengthened by many speakers : kɔ̃fɔrtaːbl *confortable*, preferaːbl *préférable*, lamãtaːbl *lamentable*, kɔ̃vnaːbl *convenable*, krwɑjaːbl *croyable*.

(iii) The length of ɛ in final stressed syllables closed by a non-lengthening consonant sound varies considerably. The student must learn the length for each word, as there appear to be no rules.

Pairs of words exist which are distinguished by the length of ɛ. The most useful of them are the following : mɛtr̩ *mettre*, mɛːtr̩ *maître* ; lɛtr̩ *lettre*, l ɛːtr̩ *l'être* ; sɛn *saine*, sɛːn *scène*, *Seine* ; fɛt *faite*, fɛːt *fête* ; lɛd *laide*, l ɛːd *l'aide* ; parɛs *paresse*, parɛːs *paraisse* ; tus *tousse*, tuːs *tous* (il le vã tuːs *il les vend tous*). In many words of this kind both long and short ɛ are heard, the latter being perhaps the more common : *laine, peine, saine, laide, vaine*.

Mistakes of English Learners

418. The above rule presents difficulties to the English learner. He invariably wants to lengthen those vowels which he associates with English vowels pronounced long under similar conditions. French i he associates with English i, French u and y with English u, French œ with English ɜ (as in *pearl*). The English vowels i, u, ɜ are associated in his mind with length. They

---

[1] With some speakers ɲ also, e.g. mɔ̃taːɲ *montagne*.

[2] Generally an intermediate a (a moyen) when long. (See § 138.)

are by no means always long, but they are always
longer than French i, u, y, and œ in the positions defined
in the rule. The i of *veal* in ˈroast ˈveal is longer than
the i of *ville* in *dans la* ˈville ; the u of *soup* in toˈmato
ˈsoup longer than the u of *soupe* in *manger la* ˈsoupe ;
the u of *duke* in *a* ˈwealthy ˈduke longer than the y of
duc in *monsieur le* ˈduc ; the ɜ of *pearl* in *a* ˈlovely ˈpearl
longer than the œ of *seul* in *c'est pour vous* ˈseul. When
the English learner hears a Frenchman pronounce *ville,
soupe, duc, seul,* he imagines he hears vowels of the same
length as those which occur in his own words *veal,
soup, duke, pearl.*

419. *Rule* 4—We have seen that all vowels in final
stressed syllables closed by the sound r are long. This
rule does not apply if r is followed immediately by a
consonant sound. The preceding vowel is then *short* :
fɛrm *ferme*, pɛrt *perte*, kart *carte*, tart *tarte*, kɔrd *corde*,
pɔrt *porte*, burs *bourse*.

Mistakes of English Learners

420. In words of this kind English learners generally
fail to make the vowel short enough. This is because
they associate such words with English words like *firm,
pert, cart, cord,* etc., where the *r* has no longer any
sound-value, but has given compensating length to
the vowel.

II. Length of Vowels in Non-Final Unstressed Syllables

421. Vowels which are long in final stressed syllables
are shorter when they occur in unstressed syllables.
The farther removed from stress, the shorter they are.
Thus a vowel which is long in a stressed syllable may
be pronounced with many degrees of length, ranging
from half-long to quite short; in an unstressed position.
It is proposed here to ignore these half-lengths and
quarter-lengths, etc., and to record all unstressed
vowels as short. Compare the following :—lə siˈlã:s *le*

silence, s ɛt œ̃n ɔm | silã'sjø *c'est un homme silencieux ;*
dɛ'rjɛːr *derrière,* dɛrjɛr la me'zõ *derrière la maison ;* il 'rãːʒ
il range, sa n vu derãʒ 'pɑ? *Ça ne vous dérange pas?* œ̃n
ɔm d a'fɛːr *un homme d'affaires,* sɛt afɛr 'la *cette affaire
là ;* il 'ʃãːt *il chante,* il ʃãt 'bjẽ *il chante bien ;* lə
di'mãːʃ *le dimanche,* dimãʃ prɔ'ʃẽ *dimanche prochain ;* tut
o'tuːr *tout autour,* otur dy 'bwa *autour du bois ;* swa'sãːt
soixante, swasãt 'sɛt *soixante-sept ;* ʒə 'truːv *je trouve,*
ʒə l truv difi'sil *je le trouve difficile ;* il a'riːv *il arrive,*
il vjẽ d ari've *il vient d'arriver ;* ʒə m də'mãːd *je me
demande,* dəmãde 'lɥi *demandez-lui ;* ʒə l ɛs'pɛːr *je
l'espère,* ʒ ɛspɛr 'bjẽ | ale le 'vwaːr *j'espère bien aller les
voir ;* la dɛr'njɛːr *la dernière,* le dɛrnjɛr va'kãːs *les dernières
vacances ;* ɛl ɛ me'ʃãːt *elle est méchante ;* də meʃãt y'mœːr
de méchante humeur ; le ku'lœːr *les couleurs,* o kulœr
'klɛːr *aux couleurs claires ;* pur lə 'fɛːr *pour le faire,*
pur lə fɛr avã'se *pour le faire avancer ;* ɛl ɛt ɛksɛ'lãːt
elle est excellente, yn ɛksɛlãt a'fɛːr *une excellente affaire.*

III. Length of Vowels in Emphasized Syllables

(a) In Syllables Emphasized for Intensity

422. *Rule 1*—Vowels which are long in normally
stressed final closed syllables are long in non-final
closed syllables stressed for intensity :—il ɛt a‖frø:zmã
'lɛ *il est affreusement laid,* ʒə sɥi ‖frã:ʃmã dezapwẽ'te *je
suis franchement désappointé,* il etɛ ‖fo:smãt aky'ze *il était
faussement accusé.*

423. *Rule 2*—Vowels which are short in final closed
syllables are short in non-final closed syllables stressed
for intensity. Length is often given to the preceding
consonant : s etɛ ‖tɛlmã (or ‖t:ɛlmã) 'klɛːr *c'était
tellement clair,* s ɛ ‖ʃarmã (or ‖ʃ:armã) *c'est charmant,*
ẽ‖pɔsib (or ẽ‖p:ɔsib) də l sa'vwaːr *impossible de le
savoir,* ap‖sɔlymã (or ap‖s:ɔlymã) ridi'kyl *absolument
ridicule.* English consonants are often lengthened under
similar conditions, e.g. ‖s:plɛndɪd *splendid,* ‖p:ɜfɪkt
perfect, ‖n:ɛvə *never.*

424. *Rule* 3—We have seen that all vowels are short in final open syllables. They are generally short in non-final open syllables stressed for intensity. Length is often given to the preceding consonant : ɛl ɛ ‖kɔ̃tãt (or ‖k:ɔ̃tãt) də l sa‖vwaːr *elle est contente de le savoir*, ʒə sɥiz ã‖ʃãte (or ã‖ʃ:ãte) d le ‖vwaːr *je suis enchanté de les voir*, il ɛ ‖tuʒur (or ‖t:uʒur) ã r‖taːr *il est toujours en retard*, ɔ̃n etɛ ‖si (or ‖s:i) œ‖rø *on était si heureux*, ʒə vɛ ‖tu (or ‖t:u) lɥi ɛkspli‖ke *je vais tout lui expliquer*, s ɛ ‖dezɔ‖lã (or ‖d:ezɔlã) *c'est désolant*, ɛ̃‖sypɔr‖taːbl (or ɛ̃‖s:ypɔr‖taːbl) *insupportable*, s ɛ ‖bjɛ̃ (or ‖b:jɛ̃) difi‖sil *c'est bien difficile*, il fɛ ‖ʒɔlimã (or ‖ʒ:ɔlimã) ‖ʃo *il fait joliment chaud*.

The English tendency is to lengthen the vowel in an open syllable stressed for intensity, i.e. to say ɔ̃n etɛ ‖si: œ‖rø, s ɛ ‖bjɛ̃: difi‖sil, il ɛ ‖tu:ʒur ã r‖taːr.

(b) In Syllables Emphasized for Contrast

425. *Rule* 1—Vowels which are long under normal stress are long in syllables emphasized for contrast : yn ʃoz deli‖sjøːz *une chose délicieuse*, ɛl ɛ ʃar‖mãːt *elle est charmante*, vuz ave ‖tɔːr *vous avez tort*, ʒ ã sɥi ‖syːr *j'en suis sûr*, kə kɔ̃te vu ‖fɛːr dəmɛ̃? *Que comptez-vous faire demain?* ɛl ɛ tu‖ʒuːr ã rtaːr *elle est toujours en retard*. This rule has no difficulty for English learners.

426. *Rule* 2—Vowels which are short under normal stress are generally short in syllables emphasized for contrast : s ɛ bjɛ̃ difi‖sil *c'est bien difficile*, il a fɛ ‖bo *il a fait beau*, s ɛ parfɛtmã ‖vrɛ *c'est parfaitement vrai*, s ɛ maɲi‖fik *c'est magnifique*, il ɛ parɛ‖sø *il est paresseux*, s ɛ sy‖pɛrb *c'est superbe*, s ɛ par‖fɛ *c'est parfait*, la‖kɛl prefere vu? *Laquelle préférez-vous?* pɛr‖sɔn nə puve l fɛːr *personne ne pouvait le faire.* The English tendency is to lengthen such vowels.

427. Thus it may be taken as a rule by the foreign learner that emphasis neither lengthens a short vowel nor shortens a long one. This does not mean that all French people always observe the rule.

IV. Consonant Length

428. Consonant length in French should present no difficulty, for it is subject to the same rules which govern consonant length in English.

429. If you compare the length of the n in *send* sɛnd with that of the n in *sent* sɛnt, you will find the former much longer than the latter. Similarly the n of *pens* pɛnz is longer than that of *pence* pɛns ; the l of *bold* bould is longer than that of *bolt* boult ; the l of *bells* bɛlz is longer than that of *else* ɛls. These examples illustrate the rule that if two voiced consonants close a syllable the second consonant lengthens the first.

430. The above rule operates also in French. Compare the length of r in *la Picarde* la pikard with that of r in *la carte* la kart ; the r of *large* larʒ with that of *l'arche* l arʃ ; the l of *Elbe* ɛlb with that of *elfe* ɛlf.

431. Compare the length of the final consonants in the following pairs of words : *pull* pul and *pool* puːl ; *don* dɒn and *dawn* dɔːn ; *kin* kɪn and *keen* kiːn ; *pill* pɪl and *peal* piːl. These examples illustrate the fact that a final consonant is longer after a short vowel than after a long one.

432. The same thing is noticed in French. The n of *saine* sɛn is longer than that of *scène* sɛːn ; the m of *somme* sɔm is longer than that of *psaume* psoːm ; the n of *sonne* sɔn is longer than that of *Saône* soːn ; the l of *seul* sœl, *ville* vil, *molle* mɔl, *sel* sɛl, is longer than that of *pâle* pɑːl.

433. The differences in the lengths of consonant sounds referred to above is noticeable only in stressed syllables.

434. Attention has already been drawn to the lengthening of consonants under the influence of stress for intensity. (See §§ 423, 424.)

CHAPTER XIX

THE USE OF LIAISON FORMS

435. Many French words ending in a consonant letter have two pronunciations, one in which the final consonant letter has no sound-value, and the other in which it has, e.g. *allez* is ale in isolation and before a consonant sound : *allez le chercher* ale l ʃɛrʃe ; it is alez in *allez-y* alez i. *Rien* is rjɛ̃ in isolation and before a consonant sound : *rien de bon* rjɛ̃ d bɔ̃ ; it is rjɛ̃n in *rien à faire* rjɛ̃n a fɛːr. *Est* is pronounced ɛ in *il est malade* il ɛ malad, and ɛt in *ça m'est égal* sa m ɛt egal. *Quand* is kɑ̃ in *quand je l'ai vu* kɑ̃ ʒ l e vy, and kɑ̃t in *quand il est venu* kɑ̃t il ɛ vny. *Les* is le in *les livres* le liːvr, and lez in *les élèves* lez elɛːv, *les hommes* lez ɔm. *Très* is trɛ in *très content* trɛ kɔ̃tɑ̃, and trɛz in *très amusant* trɛz amyzɑ̃, *très habile* trɛz abil.

436. The pronunciation which words ending in a consonant letter have in isolation and before a word beginning with a consonant sound may be called the *normal* form.

437. The pronunciation which words ending in a consonant letter have *in certain cases* before a word beginning with a vowel sound may be called the *liaison* form.

A. Words which have no Liaison Form.

438. The great majority of words ending in a consonant letter have no liaison form.

(*a*) In many words the final consonant letter *always* has a sound-value, e.g. *avec* avɛk (avɛk vu, avɛk ø), *dur* dyːr, *lis* lis, *net* nɛt, *sud* syd, *naïf* naif, *arc* ark, *hiver* ivɛːr, *air* ɛːr, *réel* reɛl, *gaz* gɑːz, *album* albɔm, *rhum* rɔm, etc. There is therefore no question of liaison, strictly speaking, in words of this kind.

(b) In many words the consonant letter, which presumably had a sound-value at one time, now no longer represents a consonant sound. This is the case in—

(i) Most words ending in the letter *n*, e.g. *maison, nation, son* (the noun), *ton* (the noun), *brun, lapin, matin, chacun, selon, quelqu'un,* etc. : *une maison à vendre* yn mezɔ̃ a vɑ̃ːdr, *brun et rouge* brœ̃ e ruːʒ, *chacun a son tour* ʃakœ̃ a sɔ̃ tuːr, *selon elle* səlɔ̃ ɛl. The most important words ending in the letter *n* which have a liaison form are given in §§ 200–2.

(ii) All words ending in the letter *m* which contain a nasalized vowel in the final syllable, e.g. *parfum* parfœ̃, *nom* nɔ̃, *faim* fɛ̃, *daim* dɛ̃ : *un parfum exquis* œ̃ parfœ̃ ɛkski, *un nom inconnu* œ̃ nɔ̃ ɛ̃kɔny.

(iii) The words *et, chaud, hors, vers, envers, à travers* : *lui et elle* lɥi e ɛl, *pauvre et effrayé* poːvr e efrɛje, *chaud et froid,* ʃo e frwɑ, *j'ai chaud aux pieds* ʒ e ʃo o pje, *vers une heure* vɛr yn œːr.

(iv) Nouns in the singular (with very few exceptions), e.g. *tort, part, sort, bras, lit, soldat, nid, drap, coup, loup, champ, franc, éclat, choix, pied, fracas, nez, Calais, Paris, Daudet,* etc., etc. The English learner is often guilty of giving liaison forms to such words. *Un incident important* is œ̃n ɛ̃sidɑ̃ ɛ̃pɔrtɑ̃, *un endroit écarté* œ̃n ɑ̃drwɑ ekarte, *un résultat inattendu* œ̃ rezylta inatɑ̃dy, *un enfant obéissant* œ̃n ɑ̃fɑ̃ ɔbeisɑ̃, *un repas excellent,* œ̃ rpɑ ɛksɛlɑ̃, *un temps affreux* œ̃ tɑ̃ afrø, *un soldat anglais* œ̃ sɔlda ɑ̃glɛ, *le nid est vide* lə ni ɛ vid, *à tort et à travers* a tɔːr e a travɛːr, *le fort et le faible* lə fɔːr e l fɛːbl, *prendre part à* prɑ̃drə paːr a, *de part en part* də paːr ɑ̃ paːr, *le sort en est jeté* lə sɔːr ɑ̃n ɛ ʒte, *Paris est plus loin* pari ɛ ply lwɛ̃ *Daudet est mort en 1897* dodɛ ɛ mɔːr ɑ̃ diz ɥi sɑ̃ katrə vɛ̃ dis sɛt, *Mort aux traîtes !* mɔːr o trɛːtr̩ ! Exceptions to (iv) are sometimes found in verse and in oratorical prose. See also § 445 (9) giving words forming part of certain special expressions. The liaison forms of singular nouns used in these expressions do not, in most cases, exist apart from those and similar expressions.

(v) Words ending in *-rt*, *-rd* (in addition to nouns of this kind referred to in (iv)) unless they occur in the interrogative forms of verbs : *part-il?* part-il? e.g. *vert, fort* (except when an adverb of degree), *ouvert, part, sort, sourd*, etc. : *vert et rouge* vɛːr e ruːʒ, *de plus fort en plus fort* də ply fɔːr ɑ̃ ply fɔːr, *fort et ferme* fɔːr e fɛrm, *sourd et muet* suːr e mɥɛ, *il part à midi* il par a midi.

B. Words which have a Liaison Form

439. Words which have preserved a liaison form are generally words which occur in close grammatical relationship with the following word, or words for which liaison performs a special function, e.g. indicates the plural, expresses a change of meaning. Thus it is not surprising to find that many of them are adjectives which can precede nouns, pronouns, adverbs of degree, prepositions, verbs of very common use, plural nouns.

440. The difficulty in regard to words which have a liaison form is that the liaison form is by no means always used before a vowel sound. Foreign students have to understand—

(i)   When the liaison form is compulsory.

(ii) When it is optional.

(iii) When it cannot be used.

441. A very important determining factor is the closeness of the grammatical relation existing between the two words in question. Liaison does not take place between words belonging to different sense-groups. Thus, while *il est bien installé* is pronounced il ɛ bjɛ̃n ɛ̃stale, *il est bien* (i.e. *confortable*) *à la campagne* is pronounced il ɛ bjɛ̃ | a la kɑ̃paɲ, the normal form of *bien* being used. *En y entrant* is ɑ̃n i ɑ̃trɑ̃, but *donnez-en aux enfants* is dɔnez ɑ̃ | oz ɑ̃fɑ̃, even if no pause is made after *en*. *Le dernier acte* is lə dɛrnjɛr akt, but *le dernier est venu ce matin* is lə dɛrnje | ɛ vny s matɛ̃.

442. Other factors are style, individual taste. In the conversational style liaison forms are much less frequently used than in the reading of prose or in public speaking ; still less than in the recitation of verse or in the acting of tragic drama. What would be extremely bad taste in everyday conversation is often good form in a more careful style.

443. The learner is advised to study the question of liaison in a more interesting and profitable way than by learning lists. He should read aloud a large number of reliable phonetic texts, noting specially the cases where liaison is or is not made. He should train himself to listen carefully to educated French speakers, noting the presence or absence of liaison forms and the effect of difference in style.

444. It is necessary at this stage to point out—

1. That words ending in the letter *d* make liaison with the sound t : *quand il est venu* kɑ̃t il ɛ vny, *un grand homme* œ̃ grɑ̃t ɔm.

2. That words ending in the letter *g* make liaison with the sound k : *un long hiver* œ̃ lɔ̃k ivɛːr.

3. That words ending in the letters *s*, *x*, or *z* make liaison with the sound z : *prends-en* prɑ̃z ɑ̃, *sous une chaise* suz yn ʃɛːz, *je veux y aller* ʒə vøz i ale, *chez eux* ʃez ø.

4. That words ending in the letter *n* make liaison with the sound n : *un éléphant* œ̃n elefɑ̃, *mon enfant* mɔ̃n ɑ̃fɑ̃. The vowel is often denasalized in the liaison form, e.g. *en plein air* ɑ̃ plɛn ɛːr. (See § 200.)

I. When the Liaison Form is Compulsory

445. The liaison form is compulsory :

1. In an article, adjective (attributive, numeral, possessive, demonstrative) followed by a noun or adjective :

les enfants lez ɑ̃fɑ̃, *des enfants* dez ɑ̃fɑ̃, *un enfant* œ̃n ɑ̃fɑ̃, *les autres enfants* lez otrəz ɑ̃fɑ̃, *de belles images* də bɛlz imaːʒ *de beaux habits* də boz abi, *les petits enfants* le ptiz ɑ̃fɑ̃, *un grand homme* œ̃ grɑ̃t ɔm, *le dernier acte* lə dɛrnjɛr akt, *le premier homme* lə prəmjɛr ɔm, *trois enfants* trwɑz ɑ̃fɑ̃, *vingt ans* vɛ̃t ɑ̃, *cent ans* sɑ̃t ɑ̃, *quelques amis* kɛlkəz ami, *tout enfant* tut ɑ̃fɑ̃, *leurs amis* lœrz ami, *vos amis* voz ami, *ces enfants* sez ɑ̃fɑ̃.

2. In a pronoun before a verb, in a verb before a pronoun, in the first of two pronouns :

ils ont ilz ɔ̃, *nous avons* nuz avɔ̃, *on a* ɔ̃n a, *je vous ai dit* ʒə vuz e di, *j'en ai parlé* ʒ ɑ̃n e parle, *ont-ils?* ɔ̃t il? *sont-elles?* sɔ̃t ɛl? *allez-y* alez i, *prends-en* prɑ̃z ɑ̃, *nous y pensons* nuz i pɑ̃sɔ̃, *en y pensant* ɑ̃n i pɑ̃sɑ̃, *allez-vous-en* ale vuz ɑ̃.

3. In the shorter adverbs of degree followed by an adjective or an adverb : *très intelligent* trɛz ɛ̃tɛliʒɑ̃, *bien amusant* bjɛ̃n amyzɑ̃, *trop étroit* trɔp etrwɑ, *trop étroitement* trɔp etrwɑtmɑ̃, *moins élégant* mwɛ̃z elėgɑ̃, *tout entier* tut ɑ̃tje, *point ému* pwɛ̃t emy, *fort aimable* fɔrt ɛmaːbl, *assez intéressant* asez ɛ̃terɛsɑ̃, *plus avancé* plyz avɑ̃se, *pas encore* pɑz ɑ̃kɔːr, *jamais en retard* ʒamɛz ɑ̃ rtaːr.

Note—In rapid colloquial speech *assez*, *pas*, *plus*, *jamais* are often pronounced with their normal form. (See § 446 (5).)

4. In *est*, *sont*, *était*, *étaient* : *il est intelligent* il ɛt ɛ̃tɛliʒɑ̃, *il est entré* il ɛt ɑ̃tre, *c'est à vous* s ɛt a vu, *ils sont occupés* il sɔ̃t ɔkype, *il était entré* il etɛt ɑ̃tre, *ils étaient en Amérique* ilz etɛt ɑ̃ amerik.

Note—After other parts of *être* liaison is usually made, but it is not obligatory in conversation. (See § 446 (1).)

5. In *ont*, *avait*, *avaient* liaison may be considered compulsory for the foreign learner, though some French people do not make it (especially in the case of *avait* and *avaient*) in rapid colloquial speech : *ils ont entendu* ilz ɔ̃t ɑ̃tɑ̃dy, *il avait entendu* il avɛt ɑ̃tɑ̃dy, *il avait une maison à la campagne* il avɛt yn mezɔ̃ a la kɑ̃paɲ, *ils*

avaient entendu ilz avɛt ãtãdy. (See § 446 (1) for other parts of *avoir*.)

6. In the short prepositions : *en hiver* ãn ivɛːr, *dans un mois* dãz œ̃ mwɑ, *sans un sou* sãz œ̃ su, *dès à présent* dɛz a prezã, *chez elle* ʃez ɛl, *chez eux* ʃez ø. (Before other words the liaison form of *chez* is not obligatory, e.g. *chez Alphonse* may be pronounced either ʃez alfõːs or ʃe alfõːs.)

7. In the conjunction *quand* : *quand il est venu* kãt il ɛ vny, *quand on a beaucoup à faire* kãt õn a boku(p) a fɛːr.

Note—*Quand*, used interrogatively, is not usually linked with the following word : *quand est-il arrivé?* kã ɛt il arive?

8. In *dont* : *la chose dont il a parlé* la ʃoz dõt il a parle.

9. In certain words forming part of special expressions. We have seen (§ 438 (*b*) (iv)) that the great majority of singular nouns have no liaison form. Those occurring in the following expressions are exceptions. The liaison form, however, does not in the majority of cases exist apart from these special expressions : *d'un bout à l'autre* d œ̃ but a l oːtr, *de haut en bas* də ot ã bɑ, *mot à mot* mɔt a mo, *pot au feu* pɔt o fø, *pas à pas* pɑz a pɑ, *but à but* byt a by, *de fond en comble* də fõt ã kõːbl, *accent aigu* aksãt egy, *pied-à-terre* pjet a tɛːr, *de temps en temps* də tãz ã tã, *en temps et lieu* ã tãz e ljø, *de point en point* də pwɛ̃t ã pwɛ̃, *dos à dos* doz a do, *tôt ou tard* tot u taːr, *de pis en pis* də piz ã pi, *vis-à-vis* viz a vi, *les Etats-Unis* lez etaz yni, *les Champs-Elysées* le ʃãz elize.

10. In those words ending in the letter *n* which are given in §§ 200–2.

11. In *un, les, des, ses, ces, mes, tes, nos, vos, leurs*, etc., before certain words beginning with a semi-vowel : *les yeux* lez jø, *ces oiseaux* sez wazo, *des oies* dez wɑ, *des huitres* dez ɥitr̩.

II. When the Liaison Form is Optional

446. Cases where the liaison form is optional are extremely numerous. If the learner uses liaison forms whenever they are optional he will certainly be criticized by even pedantic French speakers for using too many. If he uses none of them he will be criticized for using too few. Since it is difficult for the English learner to make a choice, only the liaisons most commonly made in conversation and in the reading of narrative and descriptive prose will be given.

1. In various parts of *avoir* and *être* (other than third person) the liaison form is necessary in reading, etc., and is, by many, considered obligatory in conversation. It is fairly common, however, to hear nuz avõ ãtãdy *nous avons entendu*, vuz ave apri *vous avez appris*, nu sɔm ã rtaːr *nous sommes en retard*, vuz ɛt ã rtaːr *vous êtes en retard*, ty a y *tu as eu*, etc. English people who speak rapidly are quite at liberty to use no liaison in conversation. Those who speak slowly should use liaison forms.

2. The liaison forms of parts of other verbs in common use, like *pouvoir*, *aller*, *vouloir*, *falloir*, *faire*, used as auxiliaries, are generally used in reading and are quite common in conversation. It is considered " correct " to use them, but they are not obligatory in rapid conversation : ty pø(z) ãn avwaːr *tu peux en avoir*, ʒə vø(z) i ale *je veux y aller*, il vulɛ(t) avwaːr *il voulait avoir*, il falɛ(t) atãːdr *il fallait attendre*, il fo(t) ɛksplike *il faut expliquer*, il fo(t) avwar də l arʒã *il faut avoir de l'argent*, ty dwa(z) ekute *tu dois écouter*.

3. After the third person of verbs ending in the letter *t*, except when a personal pronoun follows, in which case liaison is compulsory : ilz atãdɛ(t) ɶn ami *ils attendaient un ami*, ɛl uvri(t) yn fənɛːtr̩ *elle ouvrit une fenêtre*, il sə mɛ(t) a kuriːr *il se met à courir*.

4. In plural nouns followed by adjectives. Here the practice varies a great deal from speaker to speaker.

Much depends on the style. In reading, English learners should use the liaison form of the plural noun. In conversation it is not so necessary to do so unless a difference of meaning is expressed by the use of the liaison form. Martinon [1] gives the example *un marchand de draps anglais* which may be pronounced œ̃ marʃɑ̃ də draz ɑ̃glɛ when *anglais* refers to *draps*, or œ̃ marʃɑ̃ də dra ɑ̃glɛ when *anglais* refers to *marchand*. Nyrop [2] gives the examples *une fabrique d'armes anglaises* yn fabrik d armz ɑ̃glɛːz and *une fabrique d'armes anglaise* yn fabrik d arm ɑ̃glɛːz. It is possible to say de dam(z) ɑ̃glɛːz *des dames anglaises*, de rpɑ(z) ɛksɛlɑ̃ *des repas excellents*, də travo(z) ɛ̃dispɑsaːbl *des travaux indispensables*, dez ɑ̃drwɑ(z) ekarte *des endroits écartés*, dez ɑ̃fɑ̃(z) ɔbeisɑ̃ *des enfants obéissants*, de sɔlda(z) ɑ̃glɛ *des soldats anglais*.

Note—In *les Etats-Unis* and *les Champs-Elysées* the liaison form is compulsory : lez etaz yni, le ʃɑ̃z elize.

5. In many adverbs, e.g. *tant, autant, beaucoup, absolument, tellement, fortement, tout à fait, admirablement, franchement, vraiment, partout, essentiellement, souvent, tantôt, aussitôt, toujours, pas, plus, jamais*, etc. Some consider the liaison form of these words necessary and always use it. Others use it only in reading, etc. : *tant il est vrai* tɑ̃(t) il ɛ vrɛ, *absolument impossible* apsɔlymɑ̃(t) ɛ̃pɔsibl, *tellement insupportable* tɛlmɑ̃(t) ɛ̃sypɔrtaːbl, *tout à fait inutile* tut a fɛ(t) inytil, *il a beaucoup à faire* il a boku(p) a fɛːr, *il est beaucoup aimé* il ɛ boku(p) ɛme, *souvent impatient* suvɑ̃(t) ɛ̃pasjɑ̃, *toujours en retard* tuʒur(z) ɑ̃ rtaːr, *pas impossible* pɑ(z) ɛ̃pɔsibl.

6. In the longer prepositions *pendant, avant, devant, après, depuis*, liaison forms should be used in reading, etc. : *pendant un an* pɑ̃dɑ̃t œ̃n ɑ̃, *après une heure* aprɛz yn œːr, *devant elle* dəvɑ̃t ɛl. Liaison forms are not so necessary in conversation, especially in the case of *après* and *depuis*.

[1] Martinon : *Comment on Prononce le Français*, p. 377.
[2] Nyrop : *Spoken French* p. 159.

7. In *mais*. *mais* must have its normal form when a pause follows : *Mais | après quelque temps . . .* mɛ | aprɛ kɛlkə tã . . .; *mais | à ce temps là . . .* mɛ | a s tã la . . . When no pause follows the liaison form is optional. In rapid conversation it is generally not used : *mais il y en a beaucoup* mɛ[1] i j ãn a boku, *mais à Londres, ça se fait* mɛ[1] a lõːdr, sa s fɛ.

III. When the Liaison Form cannot be used

447. The liaison form of a word cannot be used

1. Before *h* " aspirate " : *un héros* œ ero, *des héros* de ero, *des hiboux* de ibu, *deux hiboux* dø ibu, *les Hollandais* le ɔlãdɛ, *un Hollandais*, œ ɔlãdɛ, *des hochements de tête* de ɔʃmã d tɛːt, *il est hardi* il ɛ ardi, *les huit* le ɥit. Words beginning with *h* " aspirate " are noted in dictionaries with a special mark.

2. Before the names of numbers : *les un* le œ, *ils sont onze* il sõ õːz, *les onze* le õːz, *après onze heures* aprɛ õːz œːr,[2] *cent un* sã œ.

3. Before certain words beginning with a semi-vowel : *des yachts* de jɔt (also jak), *un oui* œ wi.

4. In certain plural nouns forming part of a compound word, e.g. *chars, moulins, arcs* : *des chars-à-bancs*, de ʃar a bã, *des moulins-à-eau* de mulɛ a o, *des arcs-en-ciel* dez ark ã sjɛl.

5. In a noun-subject in the plural followed by its predicate : *les enfants ont déjà déjeuné* lez ãfã õ deʒa deʒœne, *les bois étaient tout sombres* le bwɑ etɛ tu sõːbr, *les deux dames entraient dans le magasin* le dø dam ãtrɛ dã l mãgazɛ̃. Exceptions are made in verse and in elevated prose, but the foreign learner need make no exception.

---

[1] Or me.

[2] *il est onze heures* il ɛt õːz œːr is an exception. il ɛ õːz œːr is also heard.

CHAPTER XX

THE USE OF ELISION FORMS

448. Certain French words spelt with *e*, e.g. *le*, *chemin*, have two pronunciation forms :

1. A form in which the *e* is pronounced ə. This may be called the ə-form. It is used when the words are pronounced in isolation, and also in many sound-groups [1] in connected speech.

2. A form in which the *e* has no sound-value. This may be called the elision form. It is not used for the words in isolation, but only in certain sound-groups.

Simple Examples of these two Forms—*Le* is pronounced lə in isolation and in many sound-groups : *le monde entier* lə mɔ̃d ɑ̃tje, *le français* lə frɑ̃sɛ, *pour le moment* pur lə mɔmɑ̃. It is also pronounced with its elision form, i.e. l, in many sound-groups : *tout le monde* tu l mɔ̃:d, *dans le bois* dɑ̃ l bwɑ, *Ne le dérangez pas* nə l derɑ̃ʒe pɑ. *De* is pronounced də in isolation and in many sound-groups : *le père de mon ami* lə pɛ:r də mɔ̃n ami, *la pièce de résistance* la pjɛs də rezistɑ̃:s, *il se contente de peu* il sə kɔ̃tɑ̃t də pø, *une boule de neige* yn bul də nɛ:ʒ, *un sac de voyage* œ̃ sak də vwaja:ʒ. It is also pronounced with its elision form in many sound-groups : *le Bois de Boulogne* lə bwɑ d bulɔɲ, *en train de parler* ɑ̃ trɛ̃ d parle, *il vient de partir* il vjɛ̃ d parti:r. *Chemin* is pronounced ʃəmɛ̃ in isolation and in many sound-groups : *Quel chemin?* kɛl ʃəmɛ̃? *l'autre chemin* l otrə (or l ot) ʃəmɛ̃. It is pronounced ʃmɛ̃ (its elision form) in many sound-groups : *le chemin à droite* lə ʃmɛ̃ a drwat, *un chemin plus court* œ̃ ʃmɛ̃ ply ku:r.

449. The correct usage in regard to these two forms

[1] A sound-group consists of the chain of speech sounds made between two pauses.

is in many cases extremely baffling to English learners. The name of *e*-mute by which the vowel ə is frequently described adds to the bewilderment of beginners, who find that it is by no means always silent.

450. If we regard as the *normal* form the pronunciation which a word has in isolation it will be found that the only words which can be said to have an elision form are—

1. The monosyllabic words *me* mə, *te* tə, *se* sə, *ce* sə, *le* lə, *je* ʒə, *de* də, *ne* nə, *que* kə, prefixes containing *e*, e.g. *re-* rə-.

2. Words with *e* in the initial syllable, e.g. *semaine* səmɛn, *demain* dəmɛ̃, *fenêtre* fənɛːtr̩, *retour* rətuːr.

451. The first type of words may conveniently be referred to in this chapter as Class I words, the second type as Class II words.

452. Words like *lierai* lire, *oublierai* ublire, *jugement* ʒyʒmã, *dureté* dyrte, *naïveté* naivte, *matelot* matlo, *acheter* aʃte, etc., are not properly speaking examples of elision forms, since the *only* form of these words in ordinary educated French speech [1] is without ə, both in isolation and in no matter what position they occur in connected speech. The *e* is really *mute* in such words.

453. In some words containing the letter *e* in a non-initial syllable the *e* is *always* pronounced ə : there is no elision form, e.g. *chapelier* ʃapəlje, *justement* ʒystəmã, *simplement* sɛ̃pləmã.

454. The pronunciation of words which contain the letter *e* in a non-initial syllable (like those referred to in the two preceding paragraphs) will be found recorded in any pronouncing dictionary. Such words have only one form.

455. The pronunciation of words like *table* tabl, *boucle* bukl̩, *arbre* arbr, *membre* mãːbr, which in isolation end in l or r preceded by a consonant sound, has already been dealt with in § 285 under *l*-sounds

---

[1] The *e* in such words is often pronounced ə in singing.

and in § 306 under r-sounds. Such words do not come under the same category as those of the type given in § 450, for the form used in isolation (i.e. the normal form) is not the ə-form. This normal form is also used before a vowel sound in connected speech : *une table en fer* yn tabl ɑ̃ fɛːr, *un membre acitf* œ̃ mɑ̃br aktif. The ə-form is used before a consonant sound : *une table ronde* yn tablə rɔ̃ːd, *membre du conseil* mɑ̃brə dy kɔ̃sɛːj.

456. Belonging to the same class as *table, boucle, arbre, membre* are the words *quelque, lorsque, presque, parceque, jusque*. In isolation they end in the sound k preceded by one or more consonant sounds. They have this same form without ə before a vowel sound : *quelque enfant* kɛlk ɑ̃fɑ̃, *lorsqu'il arrive* lɔrsk il ariːv, *presque impossible* prɛsk ɛ̃pɔsibl, *parcequ'il est malade* parsk il ɛ malad, *jusqu'à la fin* ʒysk a la fɛ̃. Before a consonant sound the ə-form is used : *quelque livre* kɛlkə liːvr, *lorsque j'arrive* lɔrskə ʒ ariːv, *presque fini* prɛskə fini, *parceque nous sommes fatigués* parskə nu sɔm fatige, *jusque dans la chambre* ʒyskə dɑ̃ la ʃɑ̃ːbr.

457. The difficulty which remains to be discussed in this chapter is a more complicated one. When is the ə-form to be used and when the elision form in words belonging to the two classes mentioned in § 450?

458. The form used depends to a great extent on the number and nature of neighbouring consonant sounds. Speed and style [1] are other important factors.

459. It is impossible in a handbook of this kind to make a very detailed investigation of the difficulty in question, especially in those cases where two or more words with two forms occur in succession ; but an attempt will be made to state the case as clearly as possible, suggesting, where there is a difference of practice amongst French speakers, the best course for English learners to follow.

---

[1] You will notice that ə-forms are used much more frequently in Text II (slow, careful style), Chapter XXII, than in Text I.

460. The best approach to the difficulties is not by way of rules, though the rules are useful. Listen to the pronunciation of French speakers and try to cultivate the habit of hearing the correct usage. Read aloud a great number of texts phonetically transcribed by competent observers, noting the presence and absence of ə. Prepare phonetic transcriptions for correction, studying carefully the mistakes you make in regard to ə. In these ways the habit of using the correct forms in your own speech will be gradually developed. If you are in doubt as to the correct form, use the ə-form. But the effect will be rather disastrous if you are always in doubt !

461. The substance of the following rule is often given for the guidance of foreign students. *The elision form is used if it does not result in the coming together of two consonant sounds at the beginning of a sound-group (i.e. after a pause) or three consonant sounds in the middle of a sound-group (i.e. when no pause precedes).*

I. First Part of Rule : The Rule of Two Consonants

462. Let us consider the first part of the rule, which deals with the use or otherwise of the ə-form at the beginning of a sound-group.

463. According to this rule of two consonants the ə-form is used in the case of all Class I words occurring initially in a sound-group. These monosyllabic words begin with a consonant sound and always occur before one or more consonant sounds. Thus the use of their ə-form prevents two or more consonant sounds from falling together : *le métier* lə metje, *le tableau* lə tablo, *le banc* lə bɑ̃, *le canif* lə kanif, *le dîner* lə dine, *le sel* lə sɛl, *ce livre* sə liːvr, *Que dites-vous?* kə dit vu? *je vais en haut* ʒə vɛ ɑ̃ o, *Ne fais rien* nə fɛ rjɛ̃.

464. The case is the same for words of Class II. The use of the elision form would bring two (or more)

M

consonant sounds together. Hence the ə-form : *Tenez* təne, *Remettez* rəmɛte, *Dedans* dədā, *Demandez* dəmāde.

465. In spite of the general tendency to avoid a form which would throw together two consonant sounds initially in a group many examples may be quoted from familiar conversation which show that French people often use forms resulting in the bringing together of two, three, and even four consonant sounds at the beginning of a sound-group : *je sais lire* ʒ se liːr, *ce qu'il me faut* s k i m fo, *je vous écoute* ʒ vuz ekut, *ce n'est pas difficile* s n ɛ pɑ difisil, *ce train là* s trē la, *Venez ici* vne isi, *je crois bien* ʒ krwɑ bjē. This grouping of two or more consonant sounds initially seems to be common when the first is a fricative ; and cases where initial *je* is pronounced with its elision form are particularly numerous.

466. The rule of two consonants is often broken, then, by French people ; but it is not necessary for English people to imitate them in this. Nor is it advisable to teach these forms to beginners, who, if they are allowed any liberty in the matter, will be tempted to make such mistakes initially in a group as l trɔtwaːr *le trottoir*, l sɛt *le sept*, l dine *le dîner*, k pāse vu? *Que pensez-vous?* s rɥiso *ce ruisseau*, s sak *ce sac*, l rəpo *le repos*.[1]

Important Exceptions to the Rule of Two Consonants

467. The following are exceptions to the above rule :

1. Before *h* " aspirate " *le* is pronounced lə, although the use of the elision form would not bring two consonant sounds together : *le haut* lə o, *le héros* lə ero, *le hasard* lə azaːr, *le havre* lə ɑːvr, *le huit* lə ɥit (also lə ɥitjɛm), etc.

[1] Some of these may be heard in rapid colloquial speech, but they must be considered as mistakes from the point of view of the foreign learner.

2. Before the name of a figure beginning with a vowel *le* is pronounced lə and *de* də : *le un* lə œ, *le onze* lə ɔ̄ːz (also ɔ̄zjɛm), *la moitié de onze* la mwatje də ɔ̄ːz. In naming the routes of the Paris bus service it is usual to say, for example, vwala lə a, lə i, etc. But in other cases *le* is generally pronounced l before the name of a letter beginning with a vowel : *le " l "* l ɛl, *le " e "* l e.

468. Thus the rule of two consonants may be regarded as having no exceptions for the foreign student apart from those given above.

II. Second Part of Rule : The Rule of Three Consonants

469. This deals with the correct form to be used medially in a sound-group.

1. **Groups containing only one word of Class I or Class II—**

(*a*) *The Word Preceded by one Consonant Sound—*

470. In the following and similar sound-groups in which the word is preceded by a consonant sound the ə-form must be used, since the elision form would bring together more than two consonant sounds : *elle tenait* ɛl tənɛ, *l'art de bien parler* l aːr də bjɛ̄ parle, *pour lever* pur ləve, *je suis contente de faire ça*, ʒə sɥi kɔ̄tɑ̄t də fɛr sa, *Que comptez-vous faire demain?* kə kɔ̄te vu fɛr dəmɛ̄? *Quelle est la couleur que vous préférez?* kɛl ɛ la kulœːr kə vu prefere? *Comment s'appelle le premier jour de la semaine* kɔmɑ̄ s apɛl lə prəmje ʒur də la smɛn?

Exceptions to the above are found in very rapid speech. But they should not be made by the foreign learner.

(*b*) *The Word Preceded by a Vowel Sound—*

471. In the following and similar sound-groups in which the word is preceded by a vowel sound the elision form may be used, since it would not result in the bringing together of more than two consonant sounds.

(i) Examples in which the syllable of the word concerned occurs medially in a sense-group [1] : *mon cheval court vite* mɔ̃ ʃval kur vit, *vous ferez ça* vu fre sa, *la représentation* la rprezɑ̃tasjɔ̃, *là-dedans* la ddɑ̃, *tout le monde* tu l mɔ̃:d, *la fenêtre* la fnɛ:tr̥, *le bureau de poste* lə byro d pɔst, *auprès de vous* oprɛ d vu, *il est trois heures moins le quart* il ɛ trwɑz œ:r mwɛ̃ l ka:r, *elle se promène dans le parc* ɛl sə prɔmɛn dɑ̃ l park, *Vous n'avez pas de lettres?* vu n ave pɑ d lɛtr? *Est-ce qu'on peut le lire?* ɛ s k ɔ̃ pø l li:r?

Cases where it is possible to pronounce three consonants together are given in § 481.

(ii) Examples in which the sense allows of a pause immediately before the word, i.e. where the word occurs initially in a sense-group, e.g. *nous y allons le jeudi.* (If a pause is actually made after *allons* then *le* occurs initially in a sound-group and must, according to the first part of the rule, be pronounced with its ə-form : nuz i alɔ̃ | lə ʒødi.)

If the sentence is pronounced as one sound-group, i.e. in a single breath, the elision form of the word may be used (according to the rule of three consonants). Or the ə-form may be used. One speaker will say nuz i alɔ̃ l ʒødi ; another nuz i alɔ̃ lə ʒødi. In the case of the first speaker the sound l closes the final syllable of the first sense-group ; and in this way the two sense-groups are very closely linked together. In the case of the second speaker the presence of ə prevents the expression of a very close connection between the two sense-groups and at the same time brings out more clearly the idea of each group. Similarly the sound-group *Attendez que nous soyons rentrés* may be pronounced atɑ̃de k nu swajɔ̃ rɑ̃tre or atɑ̃de kə nu swajɔ̃ rɑ̃tre ; *J'aime mieux ne pas y aller* ʒ ɛm mjø n pɑz i ale or ʒ ɛm mjø nə pɑz i ale ; *Elle m'a chargé de vous inviter* ɛl m a ʃarʒe d vuz ɛ̃vite or ɛl m a ʃarʒe də vuz

---

[1] See footnote, page 133.

ɛ̃vite. What is the foreign learner to do? If his style is ordinary conversational he may *follow the rule* and use the elision form in the position in question. If he speaks slowly, either because he has not attained fluency or because the subject matter requires a careful delivery, he should use the ə-form.

In the following examples which are of a conversational nature the elision form only is given : *Ne leur racontez rien de cette affaire là* nə lœr rakõte rjɛ̃ d sɛt afɛr la, *J'ai été occupé ce matin* ʒ e ete ɔkype s matɛ̃, *J'aime mieux ne pas le faire* ʒ ɛm mjø n pɑ l fɛːr, *Où voulez-vous que nous les mettions?* u vule vu k nu le mɛtjõ? *Comment voulez-vous que nous fassions ça?* kɔmɑ̃ vule vu k nu fasjõ sa? *Est-il content de son voyage?* ɛt il kõtɑ̃ d sõ vwaja:ʒ? *Je suis heureux de vous voir* ʒə sɥiz œrø d vu vwaːr, *Qu'est-ce que c'est que cette histoire?* k ɛ s kə s ɛ k sɛt istwaːr? *Rentrez chez vous le plus vite possible* rɑ̃tre ʃe vu l ply vit pɔsibl.

2. Groups in which two or more words with an elision form occur in succession

(a) First and Second Words of the Group—

472. Since, according to the rule of two consonants, the ə-form must be used in the first word, the second may have its elision form if this does not bring together more than two consonants : *le retour* lə rtuːr, *le chemin à droite* lə ʃmɛ̃ a drwɑt, *je ne sais pas* ʒə n se pɑ, *Ne le dérangez pas* nə l derɑ̃ʒe pɑ, *Que demandez-vous?* kə dmɑ̃de vu? *Que regardez-vous?* kə rgarde vu? *Je demande* ʒə dmɑ̃:d.

473. Instead of using the ə-form of the first word and the elision form of the second, many French speakers use the elision form of the first (thus not observing the rule of two consonants) and the ə-form of the second. This is often done in quick conversation when the initial consonant is a fricative : ʒ dəmɑ̃:d, s pəti liːvr, ʒ tə kõsɛj də l fɛːr, etc. This practice need not be followed by English learners.

474. Exceptions to the rule of three consonants will be found in § 481.

(b) First Word Preceded by one Consonant Sound—

475. In the following and similar sound-groups in which the first word is preceded by a consonant sound, the ə-form of the first word is used (according to the rule of three consonants), and the elision form of the second, if this does not result in the coming together of more than two consonant sounds : *elle se repose* ɛl sə rpoːz, *je serai contente de le faire* ʒə sre kõtãːt də l fɛːr, *elle ne me parlait pas* ɛl nə m parlɛ pɑ, *pour te le dire* pur tə l diːr, *par ce chemin* par sə ʃmɛ̃, *pour te demander* pur tə dmãde.

(c) First Word Preceded by a Vowel Sound—

476. In the following sound-groups and similar ones in which the first word is preceded by a vowel sound, the elision form of the first word may be used, the ə-form of the second, and so on alternately.

(i) Examples in which the first word occurs medially in a sense-group : *vous ne me voyez pas* vu n mə vwaje pɑ, *si je te voyais* si ʒ tə vwajɛ, *Faites attention à ce que vous dites* fɛtz atãsjõ a s kə [1] vu dit, *tout ce que nous pouvons* tu s kə [1] nu puvõ, *quand je me souviens* kã ʒ mə suvjɛ̃, *si je te le dis* si ʒ tə l di, *tout ce que je disais* tu s kə [1] ʒ dizɛ, *nous ne le regrettons pas* nu n lə rgrɛtõ pɑ.

(ii) Examples in which the sense allows of a pause immediately before the first word, i.e. where the first word occurs initially in a sense-group, e.g. *Veux-tu que je reste ici?* (If a pause is actually made after *tu*, then *que* occurs initially in a sound-group and has its ə-form : vø ty | kə ʒ rɛst isi?) If no pause is made after *tu*, *que* may be pronounced with its elision form (according to the rule of three consonants) or with its ə-form : vø ty k ʒə rɛst isi? or vø ty kə ʒ rɛst isi? The

---

[1] *ce que* is generally pronounced s kə, even initially in a sound-group.

elision form of the first word of a non-initial sense-group is generally used in ordinary conversation if the preceding word ends in a vowel sound. The use of the ə-form of the word in this position is common in reading and in rather careful speech.

The following examples are recorded in both ways. The reader must choose according to his speed and style : *il est beaucoup plus joli que le salon* il ɛ boku ply ʒɔli k lə salɔ̃, also . . . . . . kə l salɔ̃ ; *Faisons ce que tu veux* fəzɔ̃ s kə ty vø, also . . . sə kə ty vø ; *je comprends bien ce que vous me dites* ʒə kɔ̃prɑ̃ bjɛ̃ s kə vu m dit, also . . . sə kə vu m dit ; *Que voulez-vous que je fasse?* kə vule vu k ʒə fas? also . . . kə ʒ fas? *il n'a pas l'intention de te quitter* il n a pɑ l ɛ̃tɑ̃sjɔ̃ d tə kite, also . . . də t kite ; *elle sait que je ne reviendrai pas* ɛl se k ʒə n rəvjɛ̃dre pɑ, also ɛl se kə ʒ nə rvjɛ̃dre pɑ ; *il faut que je le fasse* il fo k ʒə l fas, also il fo kə ʒə l fas, also il fo kə ʒ lə fas ; *vous savez que le premier est fini* vu save k lə prəmje ɛ fini, also vu save kə l prəmje ɛ fini ; *il ne peut pas s'empêcher de le faire* il nə pø pɑ s ɑ̃pɛʃe d lə fɛːr, also . . . s ɑ̃pɛʃe də l fɛːr ; *veux-tu que je te le dise?* vø ty k ʒə t lə diːz? also vø ty kə ʒ tə l diːz?

477. It has been shown that speed and style may lead to the use of the ə-form in the first word and of the elision form of the second in groups in which the first word is preceded by a vowel sound. The following points should also be noticed.

478. If the second word concerned is *ne*, this word often has its elision form instead of the first word. The reason seems to be that because the idea of negation is not generally contained in the *ne* alone, but is expressed clearly by the *pas, plus, point,* etc. which follow, *ne* may be contracted without risk of loss of meaning. Thus it is possible to pronounce *si je ne le vends pas* si ʒə n lə vɑ̃ pɑ instead of si ʒ nə l vɑ̃ pɑ ; *si je ne reviens pas* si ʒə n rəvjɛ̃ pɑ instead of si ʒ nə rvjɛ̃ pɑ ; *il nous dit de ne pas y aller* il nu di də n pɑz i ale instead of il nu di d nə pɑz i ale ; *tâchez de ne pas l'abîmer* taʃe

də n pɑ l abime instead of taʃe d nə pɑ l abime; *je promets de ne pas le faire* ʒə prɔmɛ də n pɑ l fɛːr instead of ʒə prɔmɛ d nə pɑ l fɛːr. Both ways are possible, but the first is more usual.

479. If the second word concerned is the pronoun-object *le*, there is a strong tendency to use its elision form and the ə-form of the preceding word, e.g. *on me le montre* is often pronounced ɔ̃ mə l mɔ̃ːtr̩ instead of ɔ̃ m lə mɔ̃ːtr̩; *si je le rencontrais* is often pronounced si ʒə l rɑ̃kɔ̃trɛ instead of si ʒ lə rɑ̃kɔ̃trɛ; *nous te le donnons* is often nu tə l dɔnɔ̃ instead of nu t lə dɔnɔ̃; *j'ai promis de le faire* is often ʒ e prɔmi də l fɛːr instead of ʒ e prɔmi d lə fɛːr. Both forms are possible, but the first is more usual.

480. When a word of Class I (other than *ne*) is followed by a word of Class II the latter is often pronounced with its elision form and the monosyllabic word with its ə-form, e.g. *on se demande* is often pronounced ɔ̃ sə dmɑ̃ːd instead of ɔ̃ s dəmɑ̃ːd; *on se repose* ɔ̃ sə rpoːz instead of ɔ̃ s rəpoːz; *en se levant* ɑ̃ sə lvɑ̃ instead of ɑ̃ s ləvɑ̃; *on le devine* ɔ̃ lə dvin instead of ɔ̃ l dəvin; *il n'avait pas le temps de regagner sa place* il n avɛ pɑ l tɑ̃ də rgɑɲe sa plas instead of il n avɛ pɑ l tɑ̃ d rəgɑɲe sa plas. Both forms are possible; the first is more usual.

481. **Exceptions to the Rule of Three Consonants**

1. It is often possible to use an elision form resulting in the falling together of three or even four consonant sounds, when the last consonant sound is r or l: *un secret* œ̃ skrɛ, *ne le blâme pas* nə l blɑːm pɑ, *elle sait bien le français* ɛl se bjɛ̃ l frɑ̃sɛ, *dans ce train là* dɑ̃ s trɛ̃ la, *nous reprenons* nu rprənɔ̃. It is no more difficult for a Frenchman to manage such groups of consonants than to manage similar groups which constantly occur in his language and which he cannot avoid by inserting ə: *obscur* ɔpskyːr, *extrême* ɛkstrɛːm, *des jours splendides de* ʒur splɑ̃did.

2. It is often possible to use an elision form which throws three consonant sounds together when the third is j, ɥ, or w occurring with the second consonant in a different word from the first : *un tas de fiacres* œ̃ tɑ
d fjakɽ, *elle ne me voit pas* ɛl nə m vwa pɑ, *dans le bois* dɑ̃ l bwɑ, *beaucoup de nuages* boku d nɥa:ʒ. If all three consonants occur in the same word the ə-form must in most cases be used : *nous devions* nu dəvjɔ̃, *vous teniez* vu tənje, *un denier* œ̃ dənje.

3. When *de* occurs after words like *table, arbre,* etc. (pronounced with the terminations -blə, -brə, etc.), it is generally pronounced də, although the use of the elision form would not bring together more than two consonant sounds : *les œuvres de Molière* lez œ:vrə də mɔljɛ:r, *les arbres de mon jardin* lez arbrə də mɔ̃ ʒardɛ̃, *un membre de l'association* œ̃ mɑ̃:brə də l asɔsjasjɔ̃, *une règle de la maison* yn rɛglə də la məzɔ̃, *la table de la salle-à-manger* la tablə də la sal a mɑ̃ʒe.

4. The following are of the nature of exceptions. They are words which have no elision form. The foreign learner is sometimes tempted to provide them with one, since such a form would not throw more than two consonants together if it were used after a vowel sound : *un bedau* is pronounced œ̃ bədo, *la femelle* la fəmɛl, *il est penaud* il ɛ pəno. Other words of this type are *benêt, peler, peser, besace.* Most of them are uncommon words which would be difficult to recognize in a contracted form.

482. The reader is asked finally to note the following points about words like *revenir, retenir, rejeter, relever, reprenez, devenir, redemander,* which are formed by prefixing the syllable *re* or *de* to a verb containing *e* in the first syllable (i.e. to a Class II word) :—

1. In isolation the prefix is pronounced with its ə-form ; the verb with its elision form, unless, as in the case of *reprenez,* this would bring three consonant sounds together : rəvni:r, rətni:r, rəʒte, rəlve, rəprəne, dəvni:r, rədmɑ̃de.

2. The forms used in isolation must be used after a consonant sound : *pour retenir la chose* pur rətnir la ʃoːz, *je n'ai pas le temps de revenir* ʒə n e pɑ l tɑ̃ d rəvniːr, *il vient de revenir* il vjɛ̃ d rəvniːr.

3. After a vowel sound it is possible, according to the rule of three consonants, to use the elision form of the prefix and the ə-form of the verb : *en revenant* ɑ̃ rvənɑ̃, *en retenant* ɑ̃ rtənɑ̃, *si vous retenez* si vu rtəne, *si vous revenez* si vu rvəne, *je veux revenir* ʒə vø rvəniːr.

483. In spite of this, it is always possible to give to such words in all positions the pronunciation they have in isolation. The important function of the prefix is no doubt the reason for this. The meaning of *re-* is much more forcibly expressed in il nə vø ply rəvniːr than in il nə vø ply rvəniːr ; in si vu rətne than in si vu rtəne ; in il vø rəvniːr than in il vø rvəniːr.

484. The foreign learner is recommended always to give to words of this kind the pronunciation they have in isolation.

CHAPTER XXI

ASSIMILATION

485. Assimilation may be defined as the process by which a sound, under the influence of its neighbour, is replaced by another sound having some likeness to that neighbour.

486. Assimilations which have taken place in the past and to which many words owe their present-day pronunciation can no longer be described as being *in process*. The English word *picked*, for example, is now regularly pronounced pɪkt. The original sound d under the influence of k has been replaced by t, which resembles k in having no voice ; *handkerchief* is now pronounced hæŋkətʃɪf. The elision of d, at some time, brought the sounds n and k into juxtaposition with the result that n, under the influence of k, gave place to ŋ, which resembles k in that it is articulated in the same place. In French *anecdote* is pronounced anɛgdɔt, k having been replaced by g under the influence of the following d ; *médecin* is now pronounced metsɛ̃, d having been replaced by t under the influence of s, after the elision of the intervening vowel.

487. Assimilations like those just mentioned belong to the past. It is with assimilations that are actually operating to-day that this chapter will deal.

488. Many English and French words are pronounced in one way when they occur in isolation and in many sound-groups, and in another way when they are in juxtaposition with sounds which have the power to influence. The word *does*, for example, is generally pronounced dʌz. But when it is followed by ʃ as in *she* ʃi, z is replaced by a sound which is ʃ-like in that it

is voiceless, and ʃ-like in place of articulation ; and one hears dʌʒ̊ [1] ʃi? or even dʌʃ ʃi? in which case the assimilation is complete. *rose* is generally pronounced rouz ; but in *rose show* the usual pronunciation is rouʒ̊ : rouʒ̊ ʃou ; *jeweller's* is generally pronounced dʒuələz. But one often says ə dʒuələʒ̊ ʃɒp or even ə dʒuələʃ ʃɒp. *This* is generally pronounced ðɪs, but it is often practically ðɪʃ in *this ship* ðɪʃ ʃɪp. The same kind of thing happens in French. *je* is generally pronounced ʒə or ʒ, e.g. *je vous jure que non* ʒə vu ʒyːr kə nõ or ʒ vu ʒyːr kə nõ ; *je vous en prie* ʒə vuz ã pri or ʒ vuz ã pri. But one says ʒ̊ tə ʒyːr kə nõ or ʃ tə ʒyːr kə nõ and ʒ̊ t ã pri or ʃ t ã pri. The use of the elision form of *je* brings a voiceless sound, t, into juxtaposition with ʒ with the result that ʒ is replaced by a voiceless sound ʒ̊ or ʃ. *en face* is pronounced ã fas ; but in *en face de nous* s, influenced by d, is replaced by a voiced sound ; and one says ã faṣ [2] də nu. These are examples of occasional pronunciations that are used only in certain special circumstances ; they are not regular pronunciations like pɪkt, hæŋkətʃɪf, anɛgdɔt, metsẽ.

489. It is necessary to understand that when a sound " loses its voice " it is not necessarily identical with its voiceless counterpart : ẓ and s do not represent the same speech sounds. ẓ represents a sound (originally z) which is like s in that it is voiceless, and like z in that it is articulated with weak breath-force. The main difference, then, between ẓ and s is one of breath-force : ẓ is articulated with weak breath-force, s with strong. Similarly with the pairs ʒ̊ and ʃ, ḅ and p, ḍ and t, g̊ and k, etc. The symbol ṣ indicates that the original sound s has been replaced by one with partial voicing. Similarly with ʃ̣, p̣, ṭ, ḳ, etc.

490. The process of assimilation in French may operate in three ways ; 1, It may cause a voiceless

---

[1] See § 489.
[2] See next paragraph.

consonant to be replaced by a voiced one ; 2, it may cause a voiced consonant to be replaced by a voiceless one ; 3, it may cause an oral consonant to be replaced by a nasal one.

491. In all the examples given under 1 and 2 below, the assimilation is *regressive*, or, to use Nyrop's better term, *anticipatory*, i.e. some characteristic of the second consonant sound in question is anticipated by the speaker while he makes the first.

1. Voiceless Consonants Replaced by Voiced Ones

492. The sound which undergoes the assimilation is in each case either a voiceless plosive or a voiceless fricative. The influencing sound is the voiced plosive or voiced fricative which follows. Generally the voicing of the assimilated sound is only partial. In quick speech, however, it is often complete.

Examples :—

je passe vite	ʒə paṣ vit
la tête droite	la tɛṭ droite
avec vous	avɛḵ vu
les glaces de la vitrine	le glaṣ də la vitrin
il le cache bien	il lə kaʃ bjɛ̃
il se contente de peu	i s kõtã:ṭ də pø
pièce de résistance	pjɛṣ də rezistã:s
as de carreau	aṣ də karo
place d'armes	plaṣ d arm
les gouttes d'eau	le guṭ d o
chaque jour	ʃaḵ ʒu:r
une tasse de thé	yn taṣ də te
train de petite vitesse	trɛ̃ də ptiṭ vitɛs
flèche de lard	flɛʃ də la:r
fils de son père	fiṣ də sõ pɛ:r
sac de voyage	saḵ də vwaja:ʒ.

493. Examples like the above are very commonly heard in French, especially in conversational French. It is rather important that English learners should hear

and understand these assimilations and should try to introduce them into their own speech when they have attained the necessary fluency ; not because they are essential to intelligibility, but because they are characteristic of educated French spoken at normal speed.

494. Assimilations like those illustrated above are foreign to English habits. In English a voiceless plosive or fricative is not assimilated to the voiced plosive or fricative immediately following. *Shut the door* is pronounced ʃʌt ðə dɔə. If there is any assimilation at all it is progressive ; i.e. the t influences the ð which is often completely devoiced : ð̥. Pronounce *cross the road* krɒs ðə roʊd, *get down* gɛt daʊn, *public garden* pʌblɪk gɑdn, *pop-gun* pɒp gʌn, *brass band* brɑs bænd. In none of these examples will you be tempted to voice the final consonant of the first word in anticipation of the voicing of the initial consonant of the second, i.e. to say ʃʌt̬ ðə dɔə, krɒs̬ ðə roʊd, etc. But a Frenchman, unable to resist his own habits of assimilation, will say what sounds to an English ear remarkably like ʃʌd ðə dɔə, krɒz ðə roʊd, gɛd daʊn, pʌblɪg gɑdn, pɒb gʌn, brɑz bænd.

2.   Voiced Consonants Replaced by Voiceless Ones

495. The sound which undergoes the assimilation is in each case either a voiced plosive or a voiced fricative. The influencing sound is a voiceless plosive or fricative. The assimilation is anticipatory as in 1.

Examples :—

chemin de fer	ʃəmɛ̃ d̥ fɛːr
coup de pied	ku d̥ pje
esprit de corps	ɛspri d̥ kɔːr
tout de suite	tu d̥ sɥit
rez-de-chaussée	re d̥ ʃose.

In the above commonly used expressions the devoicing is generally complete, and one hears ʃəmɛ̃ t fɛːr,

ku t pje, ɛspri t kɔːr, tu t sɥit, re t ʃose. In expressions
of less common use the devoicing is generally only
partial :—

une grande salle	yn grɑ̊d̥ sal
une fameuse scène	yn famøz̥ sɛːn
une bague superbe	yn bag̊ sypɛrb
quinze sous	kɛ̃z̥ su
coup de timbre	ku d̥ tɛ̃ːbr
un vide-pomme	œ̃ vid̥ pɔm.

496. Assimilations like the above are made quite
naturally by English learners. *Cab-stand* is pronounced
kæb̥ stænd, *loud tone* laud̥ toun, *sad tune* sæd̥ tjun, *big
theatre* big̊ θɪətə, *live stock* laɪv̥ stɒk, *size four* saɪz̥ fɔə. It
is helpful to know that the tendency to use this type of
assimilation need not be resisted by the English learner.

3. Oral Consonants Replaced by Nasal Consonants

497. This kind of assimilation is common in very
rapid speech. It generally occurs when b, d, or g is
preceded by a nasalized vowel and followed by a nasal
consonant, the nasalized vowel exerting the stronger
influence. b is replaced by m, d by n, g by ŋ.

Examples :—

un demi kilo œ̃ nmi kilo instead of œ̃ dmi kilo, *une
grande maison* yn grɑ̃n mezɔ̃ instead of yn grɑ̃d mezɔ̃, *en
train de manger* ɑ̃ trɛ̃ n mɑ̃ʒe instead of ɑ̃ trɛ̃ d mɑ̃ʒe, *une
longue main* yn lɔ̃ŋ mɛ̃ instead of yn lɔ̃g mɛ̃.

498. In the following, the nasalized vowel alone effects
the nasalization of the following consonant : *il ne tombe
pas* i n tɔ̃m pɑ instead of i n tɔ̃b pɑ, *une longue guerre*
yn lɔ̃ŋ gɛːr, instead of yn lɔ̃g gɛːr, *vingt-deux* vɛ̃n dø
instead of vɛ̃t dø.

499. Assimilations of Class 3 are not of great
importance, since they are generally the mark of a rather
slipshod pronunciation. Good speakers use them only
in extremely rapid colloquial speech. The English
learner will do well to avoid them.

CHAPTER XXII

TEXTS IN PHONETIC TRANSCRIPTION

In the following texts :—

A short upright line indicates a slight " break " (a shallow valley) in the intonation curve. (See § 374.)

A long upright line indicates the end of a rising intonation group.

Double upright lines are placed at the end of a group in which the last stressed syllable has a falling intonation, e.g. :—

mā¹mā ǀ ɛt ap¹sã:t ǀ pur ‖tut la ʒur¹ne. ‖ ɛl ɛ par¹ti ǀ

s ma¹tē ǀ avɛk yn ¹ful ǀ də me¹sjø ǀ e də ¹dam ǀ dãz yn

grãd vwa¹ty:r. ‖

Expressions of a parenthetical nature appended to groups with ‖ are pronounced with a low, practically level intonation. In these texts such expressions are included in the group to which they are appended, i.e. the mark ‖ is placed after them :—

il ɛt a¹se ǀ ã de¹zɔrdr, sə ʒardē. ‖

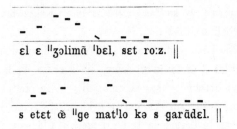

εl ε ‖ʒɔlimã ˈbεl, sεt roːz. ‖

s etεt œ̃ ‖ge matˈlo kə s garãdεl. ‖

I. Text Suitable for Fairly Rapid Reading

l εskarˈgo

mãˈmã ι εt apˈsãːt ǀ pur ‖tut la ʒurˈne. ‖ εl ε parˈti ι s
maˈtε̃ ǀ avεk yn ˈful ι də meˈsjø ι e də ˈdam ǀ dãz yn grãd
vwaˈtyːr : ‖ məsjø d veˈlεːr ǀ kõdɥiˈze, ‖ e məsjø d tiˈlãːʒ ǀ
suˈflε ι dãz yn grãd trõˈpεt. ‖ s ete ‖trε ʒoˈli. ‖ natyrεlˈmã ǀ
ˈtrɔt ǀ ε rεsˈte ι a la meˈzõ. ‖ il ε trɔ ˈpti. ‖ õn a prie ˈmis ǀ
də vnir pɑse la ʒurˈne ι avεk ˈlɥi, ǀ afε̃ k il nə s ãnɥi ˈpɑ. ‖
trɔt ɔrε mjøz εˈme ι rεste ˈsœl ǀ avεk ˈʒɑːn, ‖ mε õ n lɥi
a pɑ dmãˈde ǀ sõn aˈvi. ‖

ˈmis ǀ εt aˈsiːz ι syr œ̃ ˈbã ǀ o ˈfõ ι dy ʒarˈdε̃. ‖ εl ˈli ι œ̃
liːvr ãgˈlε. ‖ se lyˈnεt ǀ syrmõt sõ ˈne ι ε̃poˈzã. ‖ ‖okœ̃
mysklə də sa fiˈgyːr ǀ nə trεˈsaːj. ‖ εl turn le ˈpaːʒ ǀ avεk
yn regylariˈte ι otomaˈtik. ‖ trɔt a esεˈje ι də fεr ‖pɑ mal
də ˈʃoːz ; ‖ mε ‖rjε̃ n l amyz boˈku. ‖ ãˈfε̃ ǀ il ˈva ι a sõ
pti kwε̃ d ʒarˈdε̃ ǀ afε̃ d lə pɑˈse ι ã ˈrvy. ‖ il εt aˈse ι ã
deˈzɔrdr, sə ʒardε̃. ‖ il j a œ̃ meˈlãːʒ ι də kaˈju, ǀ d eplyˈʃyːr, ǀ
də gazõ ˈmεːgr ǀ e də mɔrso d ˈbwa ι eˈpɑːr, ǀ ki n rã ˈpɑ ι
sõn asˈpε ǀ ãgaˈʒã. ‖ mε tu d ˈmεːm ǀ il ε ‖bjε̃ ˈbo, ‖ grɑːs o
roˈzje ǀ ki ˈpus ι o miˈljø. ‖ sə roˈzje, ǀ trɔt ǀ nə l a pɑ
plãˈte ; ‖ il ε ‖syˈpεrb ; ‖ kεlkəˈfwa ǀ il i pus de ˈroːz. ‖ e
‖ʒystəmã ɔʒurˈdɥi ǀ il j ãn a ˈyn ǀ ‖tut epanˈwi. ‖ trɔt la

N

kõˈtã:ǀplə su ‖tut se ˈfas | avɛk ɔrˈgœ:j | e ravisˈmã. ‖ ɛl ɛ
‖ʒɔlimã ˈbɛl, sɛt ro:z . . . ‖

tut a ˈku | lez jø də ˈtrɔt | s arõˈdis | e dəvjɛn ˈfiks. ‖ il
rɛstə buʃ ˈbe | e dəvjɛ ‖tu ˈru:ʒ. ‖ ‖k ɛs kə ‖sɛ k sa? ‖ ã
vwa‖la yn ɔrrœ:r ! ‖ syr la ˈro:z | il j ˈa ǀ œ̃ kɔlimaˈsõ | ki
s proˈmɛn, ‖ œ̃ ‖vilɛ kɔlimaˈsõ | ki ‖lɛs ǀ dɛrjɛr ˈlɥi | yn
tras baˈvø:z. ‖ il turn la ˈtɛ:t ǀ a ˈgo:ʃ, | a ˈdrwɑt, | ‖rã:trə
se ˈkɔrn, | le rəˈsɔ:r . . . . | i n sə ʒɛn ‖pɑ vrɛmã ! ‖

trɔt l egzaˈmin ǀ œ̃n ɛ̃sˈtã, | pɥi il aˈpɛl ǀ d yn vwa
pɛrˈsã:t : ‖

— ˈo: ! ‖ ˈmis, ‖ ‖vəne ˈvwa:r ! ‖

ˈmis ǀ lɛv sõ grã ˈne | də dsy sõ ‖li:vr. ‖ ɛl mɛ lə ‖li:ǀvrə
su sõ ˈbra | e ã ‖katr ãʒãˈbə | ɛl ɛt oprɛ d ˈtrɔt. ‖

— k i a t ˈil? ‖

trɔt ˈmõ:ǀtrə dy ˈdwa | avɛk deˈgu. ‖ il a ɔr‖rœ:r
də se bɛt la. ‖

mis abɛs sõ rəˈga:r | e ˈfiks | l ɛskarˈgo. ‖

— s ɛt œ̃n ɛskarˈgo. ‖

ˈtrɔt | s ã duˈtɛ. ‖

— sə moˈlysk ǀ ɛ nɥiˈzibl ǀ a la veʒetaˈsjõ, ‖ vu puve l
deˈtrɥi:r. ‖

trɔt ɛ tuˈʃe ǀ də sɛt pɛrmiˈsjõ, | mɛ il a yn ‖vrɛ repylˈsjõ |
a sɛˈzi:r ǀ l animal. ‖

— ˈmis, | vu n vule pɑ l ˈprã:dr? |

mis lə rəˈgard | sevɛrˈmã: ‖

— ‖purkwa srɛ s ‖mwa ki l prãdrɛ, ‖ e nõ ‖vu? ‖ il ɛ
syr votrə ˈbjɛ̃. | s ɛt a ˈvu | də deˈfã:dr | votrə ˈbjɛ̃. ‖

trɔt suˈpi:r. ‖ il sɛ ˈkœ, | ‖kã mis a parˈle, | il ɛt
‖inyˈtil ǀ də protɛsˈte. ‖ il avãs sa ˈmɛ̃, | la rəˈti:r . . . |
ãˈfɛ̃ | il poz lə ˈdwa | syr la koˈki:j. ‖ ‖kɛl ‖ʃã:s ! ‖ l

ɛskar¹go | a y ¹pœːr. ‖ il s ɛ rəkrɔkvi¹je | ¹¹tut ɑ̃¹tje | o ¹fõ ı
d sa me¹zõ. ‖ ¹¹ply rjẽ n ¹paːs. ‖ ¹trɔt ı rɛs¹piːr | ply
librə¹mɑ̃. ‖ ¹mɛ, | s ɛt e¹gal, ‖ il n ɛm ¹¹pɑ se ¹bɛːt, ‖ ¹¹nõ, ‖
¹¹vrɛ¹mɑ̃, ‖ ¹¹pɑ dy ¹tu. ‖ ¹¹k ɛs k il fo ɑ̃ ¹fɛːr? ‖ ¹¹ɑː ! ‖ kɛl
¹¹bɔn i¹de ! ‖ il va l ʒə¹te ı par dəsy l ¹myːr | dɑ̃ l ʒar¹dẽ ı
d madam dykri¹ø. ‖ trɔt ramɛn sõ ¹bra ı ɑ̃n a¹rjɛːr . . . ‖

mɛ ¹mis | lə sɛ¹zi ı o ¹vɔl. ‖ ɛl ¹di | d yn vwa os¹tɛːr : ‖
— il ɛ ¹¹defɑ̃¹dy | də ʃɛr¹ʃe ı vɔtrə ¹bjẽ | dɑ̃ lə ¹mal ı d
o¹trɥi. ‖ sə mə¹lysk | devɔrrɛ le ¹plɑ̃ːt ı də la vwa¹zin. ‖
il ɛt ¹¹ẽ¹ʒyst | kə vu l ʒə¹tje | ʃez ¹ɛl. ‖
— a¹lɔːr, | k ɛs k il fo ¹fɛːr? ‖
mis ¹di : ‖
— e¹¹kraze ¹lœ | su vɔtrə ¹pje. ‖

trɔt kõ¹tɑ̃ːıplə l ɛskar¹go | avɛk pɛrplɛksi¹te. ‖ l e¹¹kraze
su sõ ¹pje? | ¹¹pwaː ! ‖ ¹¹rjẽ kə l ide d ɑ̃tɑ̃d krake la kə¹kiːj, |
pɥi də sɑ̃¹tiːr ı su sa ¹smɛl | la ʃɛr ¹mɔl ı də la ¹bɛːt | lɥi
dɔn ¹¹mal o ¹kœːr. ‖ õ purɛ l ¹tɥe | otrə¹mɑ̃ ; ‖ par e¹gzɑ̃ːpl, ‖
lə ʒə¹te | dɑ̃ l ¹pɥi. ‖ ¹wi, ‖ sla vodrɛ ¹¹boku ¹mjø. ‖

trɔt sə pre¹paːr ı a mɛt sõn i¹de | a egzeky¹sjõ. ‖ pur¹tɑ̃ |
il n ɛ ¹pɑ ı satis¹fɛ. ‖ aprɛ ¹tu, | lə ¹¹poːvr ɛskar¹go | n a
¹¹rjẽ ¹fɛ | də bjẽ ¹¹mal. ‖ ɛs kə sa n ɛ pɑ me¹ʃɑ̃ d lə tɥe kɔm
sa? | il sə prɔmnɛ ¹¹tu trɑ̃kil¹mɑ̃ | e etɛ pə¹tɛːıtrə trɛ ¹ge |
a fɛr sõ pti ¹tuːr | e sõ di¹ne | syr lə ¹¹bo ro¹zje, | o ¹¹bo
sɔ¹lɛːj. ‖ ¹wi, ‖ mɛ il ¹¹l abi¹¹mɛ. ‖ il ¹¹lœ mɑ̃¹¹ʒɛ. ‖ il dwat
¹ɛıtrə py¹ni. ‖ ¹eː ! ‖ ¹¹purkwa l py¹niːr? ‖ il fo bjẽ k il
¹¹mɑ̃ːʒ, lɥi osi. ‖ il ¹mɑ̃ːʒ ı sə k il ¹¹pø. ‖ sə n ɛ ¹¹pɑ pur
abime la ¹¹roːz, ‖ par ¹¹meʃɑ̃s¹¹te, k il rɑ̃pɛ dsy ; ‖ s etɛ
¹¹pars k il avɛ ¹¹fẽ, ‖ ¹¹pars k il ɑ̃n avɛ ¹bzwẽ ı pur sə
nu¹riːr. ‖ ɛs kə ¹¹vrɛmɑ̃ õ pø l tɥe pur ¹sa? |

¹baː ! ‖ ɛs k õ n ty pɑ le ¹bø, | e le mu¹tõ, | e le ¹vo, | e le

ǁpo:vrə pətiz aǀɲo | ki ǀbɛːl ᛁ ǁsi tristəǀmã, | e le ǁʒɔliz wazo
de ǀbwɑ | ki ǀsiǀflə də ǁsi ʒwajøz ʃãǀsõ? | il sõ ǁplyz
ɛ̃terɛsã k œ̃n ɛskarǀgo | e ǁpɑ ply meǀʃã | kə ǀlɥi. ǁ purǀtã |
õ le ty ǁbjɛ̃. ǁ ǀdõːk! . . . | trɔt lɛv lə ǀbra | pur
presipiǀte ᛁ l ɛskarǀgo⸝ . . . ǁ mɛ il lə raǀmɛn ᛁ dusǀmã. ǁ
sa ǀmɛ̃ | tjɛ̃ tuǀʒuːr ᛁ la kɔǀkiːj.ǁ

ǀwi, ǁ s ɛ ǀvrɛ, ǁ õ ǁty tut se bɛːt. ǁ mɛ s ɛ pur le
mãǁʒe, ǁ pars k õn ãn a bəǁzwɛ̃. ǁ sã ǀsa | s ɛ ǁtrɛ ǁmal də
le tɥe. ǁ trɔt sə suǀvjɛ̃ ᛁ k yn ǀfwa | sõ paǀpa ᛁ a tire lez
ɔǀrɛːj ᛁ a œ̃ meʃã gaǀmɛ̃ | ki avɛt abaǀty ᛁ œ̃n waǀzo | a ku
d ǀpjɛːr. ǁ il etɛ ǁtrɛz ã kɔǀlɛːr, papa! ǁ e purǀtã | lez
waǀzo ᛁ pikɔr le ǀfrɥi; ǁ le ǀbø ᛁ e le muǀtõ | brut l ǀɛrb |
e le ʒɔli ǀflœːr. ǁ trɔt a ǀvy | l otrə ǀʒuːr | yn ǀvaʃ | araʃe
o mwɛ̃ ǁsɛ̃kãt margəǀrit | d œ̃ ku d ǀdã. ǁ malgre ǀsa, |
s ɔrɛt ete ǁtrɛ viǁlɛ̃ d la tɥe ǁ e l ɛskarǀgo | n ɛ ǁpɑ ply
kupaːblə k ǀɛl. ǁ

ǀtrɔt, | a fɔrs d aʒiǀte ᛁ se prɔǀblɛm, | sə sã ǁtrɛ mal a
sõn ǀɛːz. ǁ il kɔǀmãːs ᛁ a avwar œ̃ pø ãǀvi ᛁ d plœ̃ǀre. ǁ il lɥi
ǀsãǀblə mɛtǀnã | k il kɔmɛtrɛ œ̃ ǁtrɛ grã peǀʃe | ãn
immɔǀlã ᛁ l ɛskarǀgo | a sa kɔǀlɛːr. ǁ e purǀtã, | ǁvrɛǀmã, ǁ
ǁnõ, ǁ il nə ǁpø pɑ lɛse abiǀme | e ǁdeʃikte se ǀflœːr | par
sɛt ǁvilɛn ǀbɛːt. ǁ ǁkə ǀfɛːr? ǁ il sə tɔrǀtyːr ᛁ lə sɛrǀvo.ǁ

de rɛzɔnǀmã | s eboʃ vagǀmã | dã sa ǀtɛːt. ǁ s ɛ ǁmal də
tɥe œ̃ mutõ. ǁ ǀmɛ, | ǁsi õ l ǀmãːʒ, | sə n ɛ pɑ ǀmal. ǁ s ɛ
ǁmal də tɥe œ̃n ɛskargo, ǁ ǀmɛ . . . |

il fiks l aniǀmal | avɛk dez ǀjø ᛁ epuvãǀte. ǁ ǀnõ, ǁ
ǁvrɛǀmã, ǁ s ɛt ɛ̃ǁpɔǀsibl. ǁ ǀmis | də ǀlwɛ̃ | lə rəǀgard |
d œ̃n ɛr mɔǀkœːr. ǁ ɛl a poze sõ ǀliːvr | syr se ǀʒnu, | e se
ǀlɛːǀvrə rətruǀse | deǀkuǀvrə le deǀbri | d œ̃ vjø ʒø ᛁ d
dɔmiǀno. ǁ ɛl suǀri | de pɛrplɛksiǀte ᛁ də ǀtrɔt. ǁ ǁkɔmã ǀsla |
finira t ǀil? ǁ

tut a ˈku | mis sə ˈlɛːv | kɔm si ɔ̃ lɥi avɛ piˈke ı yn
eˈpɛ̃ːgl | kɛlkə ˈpaːr. ‖ ɛl pus œ̃ kri ‖striˈdɑ̃ | e sə presiˈpit, ‖
fəzɑ̃ glise a ˈtɛːr | lə ˈliıvrə preˈsjø. ‖

kə s ɛt il paˈse? ‖ d œ̃ ˈʒɛsıtə preˈsi, | raˈpid ı e
inatɑ̃ˈdy, | trɔt s ɛ fuˈre ı l ɛskarˈgo | o ˈfɔ̃ ı dy goˈzje, ‖
ˈe, | ‖fɛrmɑ̃ lez ˈjø, | il ‖l a avaˈle. ‖

— ‖oː! ‖ ‖trɔt! ‖ fə ‖ʃɛɪm! ‖ ‖kɔmɑ̃ puve ˈvu! ‖ ‖kɔm
s ɛ malˈsɛ̃! ‖ ‖nɔtı ‖bɔɪ! ‖ ‖kɛl ɔr‖rœːr! ‖

de silˈlab ı epɛrˈdy ı e poliˈglɔt | s ɑ̃trəˈʃɔk | syr se
ˈlɛːvr. ‖

trɔt lɛs tɔbe l aˈvɛrs | avɛk ˈkalm. ‖ il ɛ ‖ply preɔkyˈpe |
də s ki s ˈpaːs | dɑ̃ sɔ̃n ɛteˈrjœːr. ‖ il a œ̃ ˈpø ı d ɛ̃kjeˈtyd |
pur sɔ̃n ɛstɔˈma. ‖ sa garguj ‖droːlˈmɑ̃; ‖ sɑ̃ ˈdut |
l ɛskarˈgo | sə prɔˈmɛn. ‖ sɛt iˈde | lɥi dɔn œ̃ pəˈti ı o l
ˈkœːr. ‖

mɛ ˈnɔ̃. ‖ s ɛ fiˈni. ‖ il dwat ˈɛıtrə diʒeˈre. ‖ aˈlɔːr | trɔt
rəˈturn | a sɔ̃ ʒarˈdɛ̃; ‖ il kɔ̃ˈtɑ̃ıplə la ˈroːz | avɛk œ̃
rədubləˈmɑ̃ ı də tɑ̃ˈdrɛs ‖ e sə sɑ̃ ˈfjɛːr | d avwar prɔteˈʒe ı
sa boˈte | sɑ̃z avwar sakriˈfje ı inytilˈmɑ̃ | la ˈvi | də sɔ̃n
ˈœːbl ı agrɛˈsœːr. ‖

From *Mon Petit Trott*, by André Lichtenberger.
(Plon, Paris.)

II. Text Suitable for Rather Slow, Careful Reading

(*a*) s ɛt yn ʃoz ‖trɛ partikyˈljɛːr, | dɔ̃t ɔ̃ n pø ı sə rɑ̃drə
ˈkɔ̃ːt ı ɑ̃ no peˈi | u l ɔ̃ sə ˈlɛːv | avɛk lə ˈʒuːr, | u l ɔ̃ sə
ˈkuʃ | avɛk la ˈnɥi; ‖ u ˈtɛ̃ːt ı lez ɑ̃ʒeˈlys ı dy maˈtɛ̃, | də
miˈdi, | dy ˈswaːr; ‖ u l sɔlɛj ˈmɔ̃ːt, | plan, | deˈsɑ̃, | avɛk
la regylariˈte | de ˈpwɑ ı d yn ɔrˈlɔːʒ; ‖ u l labuˈrœːr, | a
deˈfo ı d otrə kaˈdrɑ̃, | a la rəˈsurs | də məzyre l ˈœːr | a

la lõˡgœːr ǀ də sõn ˡõːbr. ‖ a isˡlãːd, ǀ ‖rjɛ̃ də tu ˡsla : ‖ õ
ˡvi ǀ kɔm ‖ɔːr də la ˡvi ; ‖ õ ˡva, ǀ õ ˡvjɛ̃, ǀ õ traˡvaːj, ǀ
õ ˡmãːʒ, ǀ õ ˡdɔːr, ǀ õn eʃãʒ ˡmɛːm ǀ a də ‖lõːz ɛ̃tɛrˡval ǀ də
‖raːr paˡrɔl, ǀ mɛ maʃinalˡmã, ǀ kõfyzeˡmã, ǀ e kɔm ã ˡrɛːv. ‖
ˡʒuːr, ǀ ˡnųi, ǀ nə sõ ‖ply kə də pyr ˡmo, ‖ ‖vid də tu ˡsãːs. ‖
yn klarte ˡtrist, ǀ ɛ̃fiˡni, ǀ etɛrˡnɛl, ǀ yn lymjɛːr si ˡpaːl ǀ k
õ la dirɛ ˡmɔrt. ‖ lə sɔˡlɛːj ǀ lųiˡmɛːm, ǀ kãt il dəvjɛ̃ viˡzibl, ǀ
a l ɛr d yn fiˡgyːr ǀ də l otrə ˡmõːd. ‖ il ˡsãːɪblə kə s n ɛ pɑ
‖lųi k õ vwa, ǀ mɛ sõ ‖spɛktr̩, ǀ sõn ˡaːm ǀ ‖deˡfœːt, ‖ ‖tɛlmã
il n a ni ˡfɔrm ǀ ni kuˡlœːr. ‖ il fɛ sõˡʒe ǀ a kɛlkə meˡdyːz ǀ
ʒigãˡtɛsk ǀ flɔˡtã ǀ a la deˡriːv ǀ ãtrə døz ˡo. ‖ a l ɔriˡzõ, ǀ
‖rjɛ̃ u s pųis arɛˡte ǀ lə rəˡgaːr ; ‖ u plyˡto, ǀ ‖pa d ɔriˡzõ : ‖
la ˡmɛːr ǀ e l ˡsjɛl ǀ sõ kɔm ‖fõˡdy ǀ l œ̃ dã l ˡoːtr̩. ‖ ‖kœ də
ˡfwa ǀ lə naˡviːr ǀ nə m a t il pɑ fɛ l eˡfɛ ǀ d ɛtrə syspãˡdy ǀ
dã l ɛsˡpas ! . . . ‖ e lə siˡlãːs . . . ‖ ˡɑː ! ‖ ‖lœ
‖siˡlãːs ! ‖ il fot avwar seʒurˡne ǀ dã le paˡraːʒ ǀ pɔˡlɛːr ǀ
pur saˡvwaːr ǀ sə kə s ˡɛ. ‖ il ɛ ‖si ˡvast, ǀ ‖si apsɔˡly ǀ k
õn ãn a ‖pœːr ; ‖ õn a l ɛ̃prɛˡsjõ ǀ d ɛtrə dã l pei ˡmųɛ ǀ
də la ˡmɔːr, ‖ ˡe, ǀ malgre ˡswa, ǀ l õ nə ˡparɪlə k a vwa
ˡbɑːs, ǀ kɔm dãz yn eˡgliːz. ‖ œ̃ ˡkri, ǀ œ̃n aˡpɛl ǀ vu fõ
‖trɛsaˡjiːr, ǀ kɔm yn ˡʃoːz ǀ ɛ̃sɔˡlit ǀ e kaˡzi ǀ sakriˡlɛːʒ . . . ‖
də ˡklɔʃ, ǀ natyrɛlˡmã, ǀ il nə sɔˡrɛ|t ɛtrə kɛsˡtjõ : ‖ e s ɛ
pøˡtɛːɪtrə sə a ˡkwa, ǀ nuz ‖oːtrə brəˡtõ, ǀ nu nu fəˡzõ ǀ lə
ˡmwɛ̃. ‖ də ‖tut le privaˡsjõ, ǀ sɛl ˡsi ǀ ɛ la ‖ply peˡnibl. ‖
parˡfwa, ǀ õ krwɑ ˡwiːr ǀ lœr ˡsõ, ǀ ‖trɛ ˡlwɛ̃, ǀ səlõ lə koˡte ǀ
d u ˡsu ǀ flə lə ˡvã. ‖ õ prɛt l ɔˡrɛːj, ǀ ɔ s ˡdi ǀ də pɛˡʃœːr ǀ a
pɛˡʃœːr : ‖

—eˡkut ! . . . ‖

From *Pâques d'Islande*, by Anatole Le Braz.
(Calmann-Lévy, Paris.)

(b) s etɛt œ̃ ‖ge matˈlo kə s garɑ̃dɛl. ‖ il avɛt yn figyr ‖roːz ǀ kɔm yn ʒœn ˈfiːj ‖ e dez jø ˈblø ǀ osi ˈdu ǀ kə ˈsø ɪ d œ̃n ɑ̃ˈfɑ̃. ‖· il paˈsɛ ǀ pur ɛtr œ̃ pø kur d ɛsˈpri, ‖ mɛ nu n ɑ̃n eˈtjɔ̃ ɪ kə ply ʒɑ̃ˈti ǀ avɛk ˈlɥi, ‖ kar la preˈzɑ̃ːs ɪ d œ̃n inɔˈsɑ̃ ǀ pɔrtə bɔˈnœːr ; ‖ e ilz ˈɔ̃, ǀ dit ˈɔ̃, ǀ yn divinaˈsjɔ̃ ɪ de ˈʃoːz ǀ rəfyˈze ǀ o kɔmœ̃ de mɔrˈtɛl. ‖ sa kɔ̃ˈfjɑ̃ːs ǀ nu gaɲa ˈtuːs : ‖ il parˈlɛ ɪ avɛk yn ‖tɛl sɛrtiˈtyd ǀ kə nu nu sɑ̃ˈtim ɪ rasyˈre. ‖ l apariˈsjɔ̃ ɪ də l ɑ̃ˈduːj ǀ dɑ̃z œ̃ ˈnɥaːʒ ɪ də fyme ɔdɔˈrɑ̃ːt, ǀ kɔ̃tribɥa ɑ̃ˈkoːr ǀ a rɑ̃dr a l ekiˈpaːʒ ǀ sa bɛl yˈmœːr ; ‖ ɛl fy saˈlɥe ǀ d œ̃ ‖tripl uˈrra. ‖ ‖adjø le ˈkrɛ̃ːt ! ‖ aˈdjø ǀ le suˈsi ! ‖ a rɛspiˈre ɪ lə parfœ̃ pwaˈvre ǀ də sə ˈmɛ ɪ də ʃe ˈnu, ǀ tut nɔtr aleˈgrɛs ǀ nu rəˈvɛ̃. ‖ l islɑ̃d ˈmɛːm, sɛɲœːr ! ‖ ‖kœ nuz ɑ̃n etjɔ̃ ˈlwɛ̃ ! ‖ vwaˈsi ǀ kə nu nuz imaʒiˈnjɔ̃ ɪ atabˈle ǀ a kɛlkə fɛsˈtɛ̃ ɪ də parˈdɔ̃, ǀ syr la kot d arˈmoːr, ǀ ɑ̃n aˈvril, ǀ aprɛ kaˈrɛːm, ǀ alɔr k o ˈpuǀtrə de ˈgrɑ̃ːʒ, ǀ dɑ̃ le ˈfɛrm, ǀ pɑ̃d le kaˈdaǀvrə sɑ̃ ˈtɛːt ǀ de ˈpɔːr ɪ frɛʃmɑ̃ ˈtɥe . . . ‖ le menaˈʒɛːr, ǀ le fij də la meˈzɔ̃ ǀ ˈvɔ̃ ǀ e ˈvjɛn ǀ lə rəbɔr də lœr ˈʒyp ǀ rətruˈse ɪ par dəˈvɑ̃, ǀ su lə tabliˈe. ‖ le ʒuvɑ̃ˈso, ǀ ɑ̃ bra d ʃəˈmiːz, ǀ fɔ̃ lœr ɔˈfis ɪ d eʃɑ̃ˈsɔ̃ . . . ‖ nu rəvim tu ˈsla ǀ par la pɑ̃ˈse. ‖ la grɑ̃ˈvwal, ǀ tɑ̃dy syr lə ˈgi, ǀ aʒutɛ a l ilyˈzjɔ̃, ǀ nu raplɛ la ˈtɑ̃ːt ǀ k ɔ̃ ˈdrɛs ɪ ɑ̃ plɛn ˈɛːr ǀ dɑ̃ l ˈʃɑ̃ ɪ lə ply vwaˈzɛ̃ ɪ dy lɔˈʒi, ǀ pur sɛrvir də ˈsal ɪ də bɑ̃ˈkɛ. ‖ e il n etɛ ˈpa ǀ ʒysk o sjɛl lɥiˈmɛːm, ǀ ʒysk o ‖paːl sjɛl sɛptɑ̃triˈɔ̃, ǀ ki n sə fy paˈre ǀ pur la sirkɔ̃sˈtɑ̃ːs ɪ d œ̃n eˈkla ɪ inakutyˈme. ‖ la ˈmɛːr ǀ fəzɛt œ̃ brɥi leˈʒe, ǀ ɛ̃tɛrmiˈtɑ̃, ǀ kɔm œ̃ ˈsuǀflə də ˈbriːz, ǀ l eˈte, ǀ dɑ̃ le ˈfœːj. ‖

ɔ̃ koˈzɛt ɪ avɛk animaˈsjɔ̃ mɛtnɑ̃ ; ‖ ˈe, ǀ natyrɛlˈmɑ̃, ǀ la kɔ̃vɛrsaˈsjɔ̃ ǀ ruˈlɛ ɪ syr lə peˈi. ‖ le ʒɑ̃ maˈrje ǀ plɛzɑ̃tɛːr ɪ le

gar^ısõ | syr lœr bɔnz a^ımi. ‖ õn arãʒa de ^ınɔs | pur lə
r^ıtuːr, | ã sɛp^ıtãːbr. ‖ səpã^ıdã | õ byvɛ ^ıfɛrm. ‖ l ã^ıduːj ı
avɛt ɛksite le ^ıswaf | e l kapi^ıtɛn | nə sɛ^ısɛ ı də repe^ıte : ‖
 ‖pɑːk n a^ıriːv | ‖k yn fwa l ^ıã . . . ‖ il fo sə re^ıʒwiːr |
kɔm də ‖vrɛ kre^ıtjẽ ! ‖

From *Pâques d'Islande*, by Anatole Le Braz.
(Calmann-Lévy, Paris.)